# Forever Different

## A Memoir of One Woman's Journey
## Living with Bipolar Disorder

### CHRISTINE F. ANDERSON

Interior Design Elements: http://freepik.com

Printed in the United States of America

First Edition, August 2013

www.christinefanderson.com

ISBN-13: 978-1492209867
ISBN-10: 1492209864

# Dedicated to

The Memory of my Parents;

My Brother Ricky,

Who Taught me How to Survive;

My Sister Debbie,

Who Taught Me the Meaning of Forgiveness;

My Friend Loretta,

Who Gave Me Hope;

And

My Soul Mate Stevie,

Who Loves Me Unconditionally.

A portion of the proceeds from this book benefit the ongoing work of the International Bipolar Foundation www.ibpf.org

# ACKNOWLEDGEMENTS

This book would not have been possible if not for the valuable feedback of my reading "focus" group, which consisted of my former fellow inmates from Danbury FCI; my Facebook friends; and Deb Griffith, a psych nurse from Culpeper Regional Hospital.

I would especially like to thank my support system, who also read the numerous drafts: Dr. Jennifer Oldham; my therapist, Laurel Hillstrom; my attorney, John Muldoon; my confidant, Father Michael; my dear friends, Loretta, Glenn, and Leona; and my family, my nephew, Michael, and my sister, Debbie; and my bunky, Lindsay, who already knew all these stories from our late night talk fests in our cell.

My editor, Amy E. Shelby, M.S.C.P. for her long hours correcting all my errors and making my words flow beautifully.

I would also like to thank my soul mate, Stevie, for his never-ending support and patience during the process of writing and publishing this book.

# TABLE OF CONTENTS

# Sunrise

As I am writing, I am sitting here on my bunk looking out this small
window, watching the beautiful sunrise,

Feeling a light breeze on my face and looking beyond the barbed wire fence,
which surrounds me and keeps me in.

My heart, my soul, my mind is out among the beautiful colors of the
coming day, and it never ceases to amaze me and it takes my breath away.

For it is here—it is now that I see how great God truly is! And I lie here and
thank Him every day for painting such a beautiful masterpiece in the sky—
just for me!

It is in this moment that I am truly grateful to be alive and just for a brief
moment I am free.

From the Journal of
Christine F. Anderson
Inmate: 17803-424
January 29, 2010

# AUTHOR'S NOTE

To protect the privacy of those who may wish to remain anonymous, as well as the innocent, some of the names in this book have been changed. However, the names of my family, close friends, attorneys and doctors, as well as places, locations and dates, are accurate, to the best of my recollection.

All of the poetry and quotes contained in the book were taken from my notes in my prison journal. Over the years, I wrote down quotes, phrases and poems that spoke to me, and I included in this book a few that I thought would describe the various parts of my life.

"It's not your birth date or your death date
that matter;
it's the dash in between that defines your destiny."

—Pastor Chris Harris

# INTRODUCTION

The National Alliance on Mental Illness states that 60 million Americans are diagnosed with a mental illness each year. That is one out of every four people. I am one of those four, as I was diagnosed with Bipolar I Disorder in 1987. Bipolar Disorder, in particular, affects approximately 5.7 million American adults, or about 2.6 percent of the U.S. population ages 18 and older in a given year. The median age of onset for bipolar disorders is 25 years old. One in two people diagnosed will stop their medication in the first 12 months of treatment, usually because they will experiment with their dosage and/or go off their medication altogether. According to "Suicide and Bipolar Disorder," a 2006 article published in the Journal of Clinical Psychology, 25 to 50 percent of individuals with bipolar disorder attempt suicide at least once during their lifetime; roughly 15 percent of these individuals are successful in committing suicide. The definition of Bipolar Disorder as defined by Webster's online dictionary is thus: *any of several mood disorders characterized usually by alternating episodes of depression and mania or by episodes of depression alternating with mild nonpsychotic excitement—called also bipolar affective disorder, bipolar illness, manic depression, manic-depressive illness, manic-depressive psychosis.* That's a nice way of saying you will feel so high that no street drug can compete and you will feel so low that you wish you had been hit by a Mack truck instead. This memoir is a collection of my memories and events that have shaped my life and the effects that having Bipolar Disorder has had on me and those closest to me.

At times during this book, you will wonder if it is my mania talking, and things may seem a tad bizarre and based on fantasy; I assure you—they are not. There are many secrets I have kept, and there is much people didn't know until now.

# PROLOGUE

Y ou know you're in trouble when your attorney tells you that you are safer in prison than in the real world. That's what I was told after my bond revocation hearing on January 28, 2008, which subsequently led to a 70-month federal prison sentence.

It was 9am and I was at my Pretrial Officer's office checking in for my monthly visit in the Edward R. Roybal Federal Building in downtown Los Angeles. I had the flavor of the month with me in the waiting room and I was called back for my appointment. No sooner had I put my briefcase down with my financial documentation inside it showing my earnings for the past month than two U.S. Marshals came from behind the door, put a warrant down on the desk in front of me and said I was under arrest for a new indictment. My first reaction was *Ah, Florida*. I said, "Florida?" They said, "No, California." My mind went blank . . . what exactly in California? Check fraud, credit card fraud, bank fraud, identity theft, racketeering, money laundering? The list of possibilities was endless . . . In a very meek voice, I said, "For what?" They replied, "Embezzlement." BINGO! The light bulb went off. My out loud voice said, "Shit!" My inner voice said, "I'm screwed." And with that, here's my story . . .

# PART I
# Normal? Yeah, Right.

*DON'T CLING TO THINGS BECAUSE*
*EVERYTHING IS IMPERMANENT.*
*—BUDDHIST PROVERB*

# CHAPTER 1
# THE BEST OF TIMES
# 1969–1975

I t was the best of times . . . err, well, you can decide that for yourself. I was born on September 27, 1969. I was an accident—some say I was a surprise. Well, I guess it all depends on who you ask. I lived in the Ft. Greene section of Brooklyn, New York. Back in those days, it was considered the "hood," not the trendy yuppie place it is today.

My mom was a stay-at-home mom of Irish and German background; I dare to call her a housewife because she and my dad weren't married. Hence my interesting choice of middle name: Favara. I was her eighth child. My dad was second-generation Italian American, and the owner of the local candy store/news stand. Well, actually, that was a front; his real job was running the numbers out of the back room, which I didn't find out until I was much older.

I have five older sisters and two older brothers. Or, dare I say (for they were forbidden terms in my house growing up), half-brothers and half-sisters, as they have a different father; all seven of them belong to my mother's husband, Robert Anderson. My mom and dad were never married because my mother was never able to divorce her husband.

As the story goes, Robert went out for a pack of cigarettes one day and never returned. I hear he is in sunny Florida enjoying his old age. Bastard. I mean, what other kind of man leaves a woman with a gaggle of fraggles? I never met the man, but I've heard the stories about his drinking and abuse. But I guess if he didn't leave, I wouldn't be here, so that's a good thing, right? We shall see . . .

Interestingly enough, my mother and father also didn't live together. My dad lived in the apartment at the back of his store and my mom lived at home with us. It was quite a different situation from any other families that I knew of. Hey, whatever works, right?

I guess you could say, for all intents and purposes, we were poor. My mother received welfare and food stamp assistance; other donations, such as food and clothes, came from the local Catholic Church.

The Church of the Sacred Heart was kind enough to offer each of us a place at school and subsidize our uniforms. In return, my Mom volunteered as much as she could for church and with school activities. We lived on Clinton Avenue in a three-family apartment house, and had the walk-in and second floor with a decent backyard and an above-ground pool, which was nothing to write home about. It was just a cheap, aluminum-sided pool with a plastic lining my brother Ricky picked up at Harrow's, but it made us feel rich to be the only people surrounded by projects to have a pool. We had a lot of great summers in the backyard and particularly in the pool. My father was a lifeguard back in his youth and had me swimming before I could walk. I was truly a water baby, and to this day, I still love the pool.

My memory has faded when it comes to recalling my parents, my life, and the years leading up to their deaths. The longer they have been gone, the harder it is to remember. But I do remember my father had a Hawaiian dancer tattooed on his upper right arm, his hair was silver, and he drove a Cadillac. I remember once a week, he would take as many of us out on a car ride or to eat in the city, which was always a huge deal for us kids and a major treat!

I also remember there was a period of time—about two years—that I didn't see him. My guesstimate is that it was from 1973–1975 because he went to prison for his extra-curricular activities at the store. I remember he had Dobermans that guarded the, ahem, "storefront."

One of the greatest memories I have of my father is his bringing me my first dog when I was just six years of age. My dad pulled up in his Caddy one day, opened the door, and a puppy fell out. I was so excited! Don't get me wrong—I was happy to see my dad—but I was over the moon about my first puppy. He was a Shepherd/Dobie mix, and I called him King. King was my new best friend. He was the first Doberman I had ever loved, and little did I know that this wonderful, tiny, furry surprise would have such an impact on my life in years to come.

A little bit about my mother: she was tall, broad-shouldered, wore glasses, had short, fine hair and was blessed with a quick temper. She loved taking us to the library and the movies. I also remember that she had dentures because she lost her teeth in a car accident when she was a girl, and I used to ask her to pull them out and show me. What can I say? I was a kid and gross things were cool at the time.

My mom had varicose veins that I referred to as "balls in her legs." I was easily amused back then and actually, I still am. One of the fondest memories of my mom was that she walked me to and from school every day, and she always kept a German Shepherd in the house. I adored having animals in the house, especially dogs!

Being the youngest of eight, I was raised more like an only child. There was a huge difference in age between me and sister number seven, Barbara—a gap of nine years, to be exact. I was, indeed, a novelty; everyone wanted to hold the baby, play with the baby, dress the baby, take the baby out, and show her off. Truthfully, I was all about the attention.

To a certain degree, I would say, I was spoiled and I came along at a good time, financially speaking. All of my siblings were of working age and everyone pitched in at home, but still, we were not living on Easy Street by any stretch of the imagination.

I remember most of my younger years in terms of weekends and summer vacations, a.k.a. the "fun times." My sisters Debbie, Patty, and Barbara would take me to Manhattan Beach, to their friends' houses, and to trips to the Brooklyn Promenade to get ice cream at Baskin Robbins. I felt so grown up when my sisters would chauffeur me around town!

I don't mean to paint such a rosy picture, but these really were the best of times. These were the last years we were all together as a family. We had our best decade as a family in the 70s—minus the disco, of course.

However, I was no angel by any sense of the word. I got under foot, I meddled, I tattled, I had the occasional temper tantrum, and I'm sure there were plenty of times my sarcasm was not appreciated. I got my smartass qualities from both my mother and my father. What can I say? I came by it honestly!

I recall this one time that my mother had new linoleum installed in the kitchen, and I told her that there was a cigarette burn in it because my sisters had been sneaking cigarettes and smoking. Of course, she flew off the handle and screamed at my sisters first before she asked for proof. I would never tell a lie . . . or would I?

Yes, yes I would . . . guilty as charged, even then. Of course there was no burn and I was punished for lying, but for just a brief moment, I was even with my sisters for all the teasing they put me through growing up, and I was pleased. I was such a pain in the ass, but they deserved it. They knew I hated blood and would go around saying I had a bloody nose, which in turn would send me running to my mother in tears, with my fingers pinching my nose shut.

Speaking of noses, my sisters would also kid me about my big old honker. Actually, come to think of it, I was informed by my mom that my dad didn't think I was his until he held me in his arms and saw his ginormous nose on my little face . . .

It's great to know that your dad thought your mom a trollop prior to your delivery because he was fifty-eight years old and believed he was incapable of reproducing. Good job, Dad! No, seriously! Moving along, thanks to my lovely, antagonistic sisters, I have since had two nose jobs, and now have a cute little nose, much like my mom's . . . Thanks, guys!

That's my family in a nutshell. We were an unconventional family, at best, but we were functional. A little crazy, but still functional, and it worked for us . . .

# CHAPTER 2
# THE MEANING OF DEATH
# 1976–1977

T he year of America's bicentennial. The 200th anniversary of the Declaration of Independence. These were supposed to be exciting times. I made my first holy communion that year and I got what I asked for, which was a skateboard. It was exactly what I wanted, and I loved, loved, *loved* it! Did I mention I loved it?

I also received a surprise gift from my dad, which was a gold rope chain with a praying hands medallion with the Serenity Prayer written on the back. It wasn't as exciting as a skateboard, but it was really sweet. Little did I know that this would be the last surprise I would receive from my dad.

During these times, everything seemed normal. However, that statement couldn't be farther from the truth; it was everything *but* normal. My dad was a type 1 diabetic; he was from the "old school," born on March 14, 1912, and didn't believe in doctors. He was 64 years of age, and by that time his blood sugars were completely out of control. His pancreas was failing, and gangrene had taken over his toes, which in turn resulted in his having them amputated.

As a child, the gangrene was really frightening, but what was worse was that my father was getting sicker and sicker. He started with a hacking cough that summer, and by the time Thanksgiving rolled around, he thought he just had a bad case of the flu. In reality, he was experiencing complications from his diabetes and had the beginning stages of heart failure.

After Thanksgiving dinner, my dad complained of terrible indigestion and weird pains and my mother's words still echo through my mind until this day . . . she said, "Sal, we need to take you to the emergency room and have you looked at." And for once in his life, he didn't refuse and went to the hospital. That was Thursday, November 25, 1976, and I never saw him again . . . that is, until he was laid out at Piro's Funeral Home on DeKalb Avenue for his viewing.

On December 6, 1976, I remember going to school and coming home. The house, which was normally busy with friends and visitors, seemed strangely quiet. About 7:00 that evening, after dinner and my mom's signature post-supper cup of coffee, she told me that my father died just a couple of hours ago.

I don't think any seven-year-old child quite grasps what death really means, but I was pretty sophisticated for my age, due to having much older brothers and sisters and being around mostly adults all the time instead of other children (with the exception of school).

After hearing this shocking and unexpected news, my mom asked, "Do you know what it means when I tell you that Daddy died?"

I said, "Yes, that I won't see him anymore." And with that, I excused myself from the table and went into the bathroom and locked the door. I just sat on the toilet and rocked back and forth. No tears ever formed. I don't know how much time went by before I came back out, but I remember when I did, my mother was sitting in her usual chair at the table with her hand over her mouth and she said, "You know you're going to be okay, Chrissy (that was my childhood nickname); Mommy is still here." That's when she gave me the biggest, most motherly hug of my life to that point, and somehow, I felt safe again.

What happened was that my father slipped into a diabetic coma, and the prognosis was that he would be a vegetable if he recovered. My mother prayed that he wouldn't be asked to live the rest of his life in such a state and asked God to please spare him by ending his suffering. God heard her prayers and answered them immediately.

In retrospect, I would have to agree with her. At the ripe old age of seven, his passing was, for me, the hardest life lesson to date, but it was for the best. My father wouldn't have wanted to live that way, completely dependent on others for his personal care with no quality of life. He was a proud, strong, Italian-American man and deserved to die peacefully and with dignity.

In the days following my father's burial, there was constant arguing back and forth about the store and how much, or if any, money would be left to me. Truth be told, my Uncle Joe, my father's brother, was such a selfish individual that he made sure I didn't get anything. These were his exact words: "She is a bastard child." Families can be so cruel and greedy after a supposed loved one of theirs passes.

All I had left of my father was a platinum pinky ring with diamonds and rubies and the St. Christopher medal he wore every day—the same medallion that he took off and handed to my mother the night she brought him to the hospital. It was as if he knew he was going to die that night.

You would think I would have been more affected—emotionally disturbed, melancholic—but I wasn't. The next year and two months passed with me doing all the normal things kids my age do: I went to school, played with my dolls, hung out with friends and, of course, loved on my dog. The same dog my dad surprised me with when I was just six years old. Everything was okay in my world. After all, my mother was correct—I still had her . . . right?

# Chapter 3
## The Deeper Meaning of Death
## 1978

I remember the following details so vividly it's as if it happened yesterday. There was a blizzard that year, and the winter was much colder and longer than usual. One of my many sisters, Patty, was due with my niece, Melissa, and we had a fantastic baby shower for her.

At about the same time, I remember my mother telling me she had to have surgery, and she would be gone for a few days in the hospital, and that my siblings, Debbie and Ricky, were going to watch me. She made it seem like no big deal, and she was a strong woman, so I wasn't worried at all.

Mom left on Tuesday, February 14—Valentine's Day—and they brought me to the hospital to see her that evening because her surgery was the next morning. On Wednesday, she had a routine hysterectomy. I spoke to her for a brief two minutes that evening after she came out of recovery.

The next morning, Thursday, February 16, the phone rang in what must have been the wee hours of the morning because Ricky hadn't left for work yet, and he had stated that he needed to make sure Debbie remembered to drop me off at school.

I spent the day at school, none the wiser, and I was picked up by my eldest sister, Kathy, and my brother-in-law-to-be, Tony, in his VW Rabbit. I found it strange that they were home from work, and secondly, I always walked home with one of my sisters. My mind started to wonder what was going on.

We arrived at the house, and the kitchen was full of my mother's friends, Aunts Rosy and Helen, as well as all of my brothers and sisters (with the exception of my brother, Bobby, who was estranged from the family at this point; he was asked to go see my mother in the hospital, yet he refused).

I recall Debbie, Patty, Barbara, Kathy, Suzy, and Ricky taking me into the living room and telling me that Mommy wouldn't be coming home because she died. Instantly, I felt that life as I knew it was going to be drastically different. I remember sobbing uncontrollably and holding onto Debbie as tight as I could.

Then Ricky, unknowing of the words Mom uttered to me when Dad died, said, "It's going to be okay, Chrissy; you still have all of us." I was horrified. I wanted my mom back, and there was nothing I could do about it. She was gone. Mom had complications after surgery—a clot in her blood stream caused a heart attack. It was explained to me that my mother got up that morning and packed to come home, and the blood clot rushed to her heart and killed her instantly. The only positive thought I can pull from this horrific memory is "at least she didn't suffer."

The most dreadful experience was the first night of the viewing, again at Piro's Funeral Home. It was the first time we saw her lifeless body. Debbie had to be taken out; she was completely hysterical. I remember my brother, Ricky, took my hand and asked me if I wanted to go up and see her, and I nodded yes. I had to see my mom one last time, and I had to see it for myself.

Mom looked like she was only sleeping. I reached out to touch her hand and she was just so cold! I remember that I just knelt in front of her and held her hand, praying that she would wake up and that this was just a terrible nightmare. I just knelt there, at eight years old, not saying a word, as I cried in silence over the death of my mother.

My family (what was left of it anyway) endured two torturous days and evenings of viewings, and we buried my mother in St. Charles Cemetery on Long Island. My brother insisted, of course, on a formal church mass, followed by a procession of limousines to the chapel at the cemetery where we would all have our final goodbye. He felt the graveside burial would be too difficult on all of us.

I remember two things from the mass: my entire class from school was there, and my brother gave a heart-wrenching eulogy. Ricky recited a poem he wrote for her in high school, called "She Was a Friend." My tears were endless by this time. We were all present except for my brother, Bobby, who asked if he could come at this point, to which Ricky replied, "If you wanted to see her so badly, you should have seen her when she was alive. No, you are not welcome." And so we were seven. No mother and no father. We only had each other to depend on.

All I can say is, the old adage is true—you can choose your friends, but you can't choose your family. My brothers and sisters fought tooth and nail over my mother's stuff, from her jewelry to her welfare check. In the days and months following my mother's death, emotions were high and any and all common sense went out the window.

My mother's death, unlike my father's, affected me greatly. She was always there for me and told me that I still had her, but this was no longer true. I made attempts to still feel connected to my mom, who I missed tremendously. I used to sit in the closets in the hallway, as well as the two in the kitchen, and smell her clothes, which still had the essence of her scent. I would go through her alligator purse relentlessly and try to reach her jewelry box to put on her jewelry. I wanted to smell Mom, feel Mom, act like Mom, and look like Mom.

My brother, Ricky, witnessed my behaviors and didn't feel this was healthy for me. He quickly decided that we should consider moving. He thought that the house on Clinton Avenue was filled with too many memories, too many ghosts. That summer, he took me on a drive over the Brooklyn Bridge to Manhattan and asked me whom I wanted to live with. I told him I would like to stay with him. Truthfully, I was afraid to say anything different for fear of being shipped to an orphanage or foster care.

And so it was decided. I would stay with Ricky, and he decided to move from Clinton Avenue to Bensonhurst—77th Street and 13th Avenue, to be exact. The change was a huge deal—we went from the ghetto to what is still today a predominantly white environment, so segregated you would think you had stepped back in time to the Deep South of the 1950s.

I was confused, I was young, and I was parentless, and looked up to Ricky for guidance now. I had black friends and Puerto Rican relatives through marriage, and didn't understand. What do you mean, I can't talk to anybody or be seen with anyone who isn't white, and better yet and more preferably, Italian? Why not?

We moved that summer. My guess it was June 1978. My brother was always one to get things done; he never let grass grow under his feet. He moved our things a little at a time and went through as much of my mother's stuff as possible. We narrowed a house full of her belongings down to some furniture and a few boxes.

One night, Ricky decided he would make a trip and take over some of the living room furniture—in particular, two wood chairs that were on rollers. In the vestibule between the front door and the inside hallway, we had another door; in it was an old wire mesh window, which consisted of two panes of glass and, in between, wire mesh for security. I was in the living room watching TV, and Debbie was helping him move.

At one point, the chair somehow got wedged in the door and my brother forced it, and his hand slipped and went through the wire mesh window. The worst part of this story is not that his hand went through it, but that he pulled it back out, severing every nerve and artery in his hand. I remember hearing "pop" noises, which sounded like a tire letting out air before going flat.

There was blood everywhere, and when I say everywhere, I mean *everywhere!* Ricky managed to wrap his arm in an old gold bed sheet, and Debbie drove him to Cumberland Hospital. As he was walking toward the car to leave, I heard him saying to my sister, Patty, who happened to live on the third floor of the same building, "Make sure to take care of the baby; I will be back as soon as I can." I remember thinking, "Yea, right . . . so far, two people have left to go the hospital and they haven't come back. What makes you so sure that you're coming back?" I thought he was a goner for sure. On the inside, I was panicked, but on the outside, I showed a brave face.

Several hours of surgery and on the precipice of losing his hand, Ricky wound up with 144 stitches on the outside and too many stitches to count on the inside, along with a permanent clamp on the inside of his arm near the wrist. It was his right hand that was damaged, and of course, he was right-handed. This meant months of physical therapy and a period of time when he was out of work, but we would be financially stable because he had excellent benefits as an electrician. The whole situation was traumatizing, but I was just happy that my brother came back from the hospital . . . alive!

One day soon after the hand-maiming incident, we were still unpacking and Ricky was home convalescing when the doorbell rang. He asked me to answer it and so I did. A familiar black man stood in the doorway. I could swear I knew him from somewhere, but I wasn't absolutely sure.

He spoke. "Little girl, can you get your mommy for me?"

In an extremely matter-of-fact voice and as if he were an alien, I answered, "Mom . . . Mommy's dead."

He then replied, "Little girl, that's not nice to say."

I abruptly retorted, "It's true," and then I yelled for my brother. Years later, Ricky told me that he and my mother had dated when my father went to prison. His name was Luther, and he was always fond of my mother. Apparently, when I blurted out that she was dead, it shocked him and he had to come in and sit for a while. Ricky explained to me that how I handled the situation was incorrect, and my choice of words was poor. Unfortunately, I, still the same to this day, said it like it was and didn't understand what I said that was so wrong. It was the truth, right? But as most of us have probably realized at one time or another, there are kinder and gentler ways to deliver bad news. And in some circumstances, brutal honesty just isn't an option.

Later that year it was official: my brother, Ricky, at the age of 23, had legal custody of me, compliments of the Legal Aid Society of New York. It was just him and me living in a two-bedroom apartment over a tuxedo shop. At this time, he was now working for New York University and travelling the train from Brooklyn to Manhattan every day. He was in construction now and working with a crew to build additions onto the school.

We followed the same routine, day in and day out. He would leave the house at 5am and didn't get home until 6 or 7 in the evening. This meant that I would get myself to school, come home and complete my homework, hang out on the block with my friends until 5:00 rolled around, and then I would prepare dinner for when Ricky would get home, as well as have a fresh pot of coffee waiting for him. To actually say that my brother was addicted to coffee would be an understatement.

Need I remind you that during this time period, I was eight turning nine? At no time, from the passing of my father to the death of my mother, and the transition to living with my brother, did anyone mention therapy or counseling; it just wasn't done in those days. We were, indeed, living one day at a time and, sometimes, even one moment at a time.

Ricky always did what he thought was best, which, of course, was to ignore it and it would go away. The pain, the loneliness . . . it was just temporary. Yep, that's what he said. I used to have the most horrifying nightmares, and they were always the same recurring dream. I would be at the top of the staircase, trip and fall, but I never reached the bottom. This freaked me out so bad that I would wake up in the middle of the night screaming and go crawl into bed with my brother. Ricky would then put an arm around me until I fell asleep. Eventually, they stopped, and I just went on existing. I mean . . . I was fine, wasn't I?

Christmas crept up on me quickly, and I wasn't expecting much. This would be the first year that Mom wouldn't be around to celebrate with us. My brother went right on living—he decorated to the nines like he always did. Christmas was and still is his favorite time of the year. To this day, I am unsure if he was ignoring the hurt as usual, putting up a front for me, or a combination of both? Christmas went on as if nothing had changed.

That year, I ended up getting the oh-so-cool Barbie camper. I was a Barbie fanatic, to say the least. Oh, come on, doesn't everyone love Barbie? Yeah, yeah, it was a phase. Besides the Barbie (stop laughing), I also received Sonny and Cher dolls and a Grease sweatshirt. What can I say? These were very different times, and my taste was quite eclectic.

The gifts my brother got me were really neat, but the gift that stood out the most about this Christmas was a voice recording of the Christmas prior, which was the last Christmas my mom was alive. I became obsessed. I listened to it over and over again trying to remember her voice, wishing it would remain in my mind forever. I don't recall how many Christmases since her death that I listened to that recording, but there were many. At this point in my life, I am not even sure that the tape still exists. All I really know is how I wish I had that tape in my possession now.

# Chapter 4
## Change is Good, Right?
## 1979

We celebrated the New Year just as we did when my mom was alive: eating Ritz Crackers with peanut butter and jelly and watching Dick Clark in Times Square. I was in a new school, had new friends and was in somewhat of a routine.

Sometime between my mother's death and the beginning of 1979, my brother had words with each of my siblings (except my sisters, Suzy and Patty). Debbie was banished to my aunt and uncle's in Long Island because she wouldn't obey the rules of the house. She broke curfew so many times my brother put an alarm on the house to keep her in. In her defense, she was 19, working, and shouldn't have had a curfew. Barbara moved to Long Island as well, and was soon to be married to Tony. My brother was still pissed at her for wanting her portion of my mother's welfare check after she died and, well, he and Bobby hadn't spoken since Bobby's wedding in 1973. They never got along. Kathy . . . well, the story goes like this: my brother co-signed a $25,000 loan for her and she moved to California, skipping out on the payments and leaving him holding the bag. Everyone was forbidden to see or talk to me, but they snuck calls and visits when they could. I will say my sisters made sure they were in touch and did what they could.

We visited my mother's grave often. It was not unusual for us to drive a couple hours and spend a couple of hours there just sitting and talking and reminiscing while my brother had coffee and smoked cigarettes. We never visited my father's grave. At this point, he was just a figment of my imagination. It wasn't until I was 17 that I visited my father's grave. I never understood why, if they took me to my mother's, they wouldn't take me to my father's. It's a question I still ask myself today.

It was still winter. We had been living in Bensonhurst for six months or so when Ricky came home one day and told me the good news (maybe for him)—he got a promotion and we would moving to Manhattan in the next month.

I panicked. Another new school, more new friends. This was terrible news. The most heartbreaking part of this move was that King couldn't come with us, as the apartment we were moving to didn't allow dogs. But my brother assured me he made arrangements with a nice family, the Woods, to take him. I didn't know then what I know now . . . the Woods family, get it? He just dropped him off somewhere on the LIE. I was so pissed when I figured that out when I was older.

Here we were in our new apartment, compliments of NYU and rent-free. My brother was now Superintendent of NYU's faculty buildings called Silver Towers on Bleeker Street in Greenwich Village. Let me put this in perspective. First, I lived in the ghetto, and then I lived in a time warp. Now I'm living in a building with my very own doorman in an area of New York that is so rich in culture and diverse in its ethnicities and sexual preferences I don't know how to act. So I did what any normal kid who has lost both her parents, moves twice in a year and is not in therapy does: I withdrew.

My brother tried everything to entertain me: ice skating lessons at Rockefeller Center, shopping, movies, libraries, museums, Broadway

Musicals, day camp, Girl Scouts and after-school activities. Suffice it to say I was still unhappy.

By the summer of 1979, he was at his wit's end. My sister Suzy came up with the idea to send me with my twin nephews, Joe and Mike (who oddly are a year older than I), and their younger sister Joyce to Virginia with the Fresh Air Fund. The Fresh Air Fund is a non-profit organization based in New York City that, to date, sends at-risk, inner-city youth to host families somewhere in the country for two weeks during the summer.

Now this, *this* appealed to me; a farm, which meant animals. All my nephews and my niece talked about whenever they came home from their trip were the farm and the animals. Okay, I'm in.

We departed from the Port Authority at some ungodly hour of the morning on a Greyhound bus chartered for the Fresh Air Fund with about 30 kids headed out of New York City for two weeks. Very exciting, I'm telling you. Next stop: Madison, Virginia.

My host family was a nice family from Culpepper, and they had a daughter my age named Bobbie and an older daughter (her name escapes me). We got to their place, which was a wonderful farm house on several acres about a half-hour drive from where the bus dropped us off. Guess what? No animals—just a dog. I could have stayed home for this. This was no farm, just a nice house with some land. I did mention they were nice, right? Well, a few days into my first week, I was homesick and all I did was cry. The family called the area coordinators, a wonderful Mennonite family by the name of Miller. The Millers also happened to be the host family for my nephew Michael, and they agreed to pick me up and let me stay with them for the remainder of the vacation. Thank God! I was so happy. One, I would be with family, and two, I was going to a real farm!

When I got to the Millers', I was happier than a pig in shit, no pun intended. There were animals everywhere—cows, pigs, chickens, ponies, dogs, cats, and yes, bunnies. Even then I knew I was in my element. I was so enthralled by all the animals it was almost overwhelming at first. The

Millers had six children, plus a couple of Fresh Air kids. It was a busy place and they were dairy farmers. There were plenty of chores and activities for us to all do, so we weren't bored. And although, due to religious reasons, there was no TV and no radio, I couldn't have cared less.

I fell in love with a little bunny that couldn't have been more than a few weeks old. I named him Thumper. Sadly (and I hate to admit this), I suffocated him to death. I held him so tight and often that at some point I cut off his breathing. The Millers didn't think anything of it. I, on the other hand, was devastated. This obviously threw a monkey wrench into my plans (I was going to take him home to New York, sneak him on the Greyhound and keep him in a shoebox in my room—unbeknownst to my brother, of course).

During the week, the Millers sent us to vacation Bible School at the Oak Grove Mennonite Church. It was now my second week into the vacation and I was learning about the Bible and Jesus. At lunch, I met the person who will forever be my sister by choice—Loretta.

Michelle Ventor once said, "People come into your life for a reason, a season, or a lifetime. When you figure out which it is you know exactly what to do." In an instant, Loretta was my summer sister. We got along like "peas and carrots," as Forrest Gump would say. We were inseparable that week, so much so that Loretta asked her parents if they could be my host family next summer, and the plans were made for my return.

Loretta and I became pen pals. This is when writing a letter and mailing it was still an art. We wrote weekly and the letters talked about boys and friends and things we were doing, and about what we were going to do the next summer.

From 1979 to 1985, I spent every summer vacation and sometimes my winter break at the Overholt's' Dairy Farm in Aroda, Virginia. The Overholt family was then, and still is now, the most generous people I know. They took us on trips to see the National Zoo in DC, Monticello, Thomas Jefferson's home, Busch Gardens, Skyline Drive and Big Meadows in the Blue Ridge Mountains, the Grand Caverns. But some of my best memories were some of the simplest things we did, like sleeping out on the trampoline on a cool night under the stars, when the sky was so clear, unlike the city. On hot days, we would swim in the creek, or just sit at the edge and dip our toes. Or when we used to come in from Bible School and split a half gallon of heavenly hash ice cream between all of us kids. We did farm stuff. Loretta had chores and I helped, which I always thought was really cool. We'd milk the cows, feed the chickens, get fresh eggs, drink milk straight from the cow, and pick berries.

Now, here is what I found in Virginia during the summers that made everything right with the world . . . horses. It was love at first sight. The first horse I ever rode was borrowed from Loretta's neighbor, Delores—an Appaloosa named Scooby. Well, there are no words to describe the connection between the horse and his rider. You are one. Winston Churchill said it best: "The outside of a horse is good for the inside of a man." It won't be until later in this book that we see how these words ring true.

# CHAPTER 5
# LIKE, TOTALLY 80S, DUDE
# 1980–1985

I was attending St. Anthony's School in New York City and by this time, I was 11 years old and in the sixth grade. I loved it in Manhattan despite my whining and sniveling about the move. I had lots of friends and I loved being in the city. I especially loved the summers in the city when all of the Catholic parishes would have their feast and we stayed out late in Thompson Street Park, listening to music and dancing and carrying on being kids.

My brother was strict. I had to be in by 7:30pm during the week and 9pm on the weekends. Needless to say, I was the only one who had this ridiculous curfew. I seriously ran home as soon as the street lights came on. Getting a bike made getting to and from much faster later on.

My sister Debbie was living in Long Island, at her uncle Don's (her father's brother), and was preparing for her wedding. She had since patched things up with my brother; she was on his good side again. She used to take me on weekends for a couple weeks out of the summer. I loved going out to see them—we always did such fun stuff, like roller skating with my step-cousins Timothy and Michael, and going to a kid's disco, Bugsy Malone's. We also would walk to a park nearby on Lincoln Avenue in Holbrook, where she lived, and spend a lot of time in the summer in their pool or playing volleyball in the backyard.

It's right about this time I started to develop the Sunday Night Blues, as I called them. Experts would say night terrors. I would fear going to school on Monday to the point that I would fake sick and asked to be taken to the emergency room. It wasn't that I didn't like school or was afraid of something. Here is where I'd like to tell you something started to seem a little off, and I just felt safer in my room or in the apartment. The experts say those were the first signs of being paranoid, or terrors, which can be at night or during the day, a symptom in the early onset of adolescent Bipolar Disorder. Of course, I just shrugged it off and didn't say anything to anyone, for fear they would think I was crazy and send me to Bellevue.

It's now 1981. During this time, I started spending most of my weekends at my sister Suzy's, and with my nephews Joe and Mike, and my niece Joyce. Back in those days, we were inseparable. My brother bought a three-family house on Bay 46th Street in the Bensonhurst section of Brooklyn, and my sister had the walk-in four-bedroom apartment. Joe, Mike and Joyce were more like my brothers and sisters than my real ones because we were closer in age. It was a 40-minute ride on the B train from the Broadway/Lafayette Station in Manhattan to the Bay 50th Street stop in Brooklyn. I had friends there also—I have great memories or my two friends, Rita and Roxanne. We experimented with hair, makeup and fashion. My sister was a lot more liberal than my brother, so we had no curfew, and this was awesome!

We did other kinds of experimenting, too; this was our first experience of drinking. There was a feast on Harway Avenue at the Church of the Most Precious Blood. I looked old for my age and I decided I was going to try to gamble to win a bottle of red wine on the roulette wheel, and I did. In fact I won two, and I sat down and I drank them, both of them. I was 12, and of average size. Forget the fact that a couple of hours later and the next two days, I vomited. I could have had alcohol poisoning and killed myself. Of course, I swore everyone to secrecy and said I had the flu. Had I said something, I'm sure I would have been brought to have my stomach pumped. It would be ten years before I took another sip of red wine; in fact, just the smell of it made me want to hurl. Incidentally, I had my real French first kiss on this night but I barely remember it.

The 80s are rolling right along and we're into 1982. I am 13 when my brother meets a woman he decides to marry, Faye. All I can say is she was fine before he put the ring on her finger. After they said "I do" and she moved in, she turned into Cruella Deville. I mean, this lady made me miserable. She had a terrific family that lived on Staten Island, and I enjoyed spending Sundays having a nice, big Italian meal and sitting around talking, but the good didn't outweigh the bad in this particular instance. I hated her and she hated me, which made things interesting for my brother, as he constantly was in the middle playing referee. I'm not saying we were at each other's throats all the time, but it was more often than not. Truth be told, we were jealous of each other and that made for an unhappy coexistence. She would do stuff that reminded me of a wicked stepmother, like doing her and my brother's laundry but making me do my own. I was 12 and knew how to do laundry—I'd been doing it since I was eight—but this was so not the point.

It was 1984, he was still married to Cruella, and I was graduating from St. Anthony's, having been accepted into a private all-girls Catholic high school, Notre Dame Academy, on the Upper East Side of Manhattan. I was looking forward to the summer and letting off some steam before things got serious and I started high school. Then my brother hit me with the news: he found a better job as a Director of Housekeeping (nice word for head janitor) at the Village Nursing Home on the West Side and we would have to move because he couldn't keep the apartment if he didn't work for NYU anymore. Here we go again. Another move. New friends. Hey, I was getting good at this by now.

Off to Staten Island we went. My brother bought a nice ranch-style home with an in-ground pool in the Annandale section of Staten Island. I have to admit, this was a pretty cool house. It had a bookcase that pulled out and behind it were the stairs to the basement. My room was in the attic, which was, surprisingly, my choice and not Cruella's. My room had hideaway storage doors and built-in furniture—very cool. However, I was determined not to lose my foothold on Manhattan, so along with my brother, Cruella and her father, I drove into Manhattan every day, which was at least a two-hour commute with traffic on a good day, and continued to attend Notre Dame. I have to tell you, I am not a morning person and getting up at the crack of dawn was not going over well with me. After my freshman year, I gave up Manhattan and opted to attend school at Tottenville High School on Staten Island.

I would have to liken the difference between Manhattan and Staten Island to going from Las Vegas to the Ozarks now. I mean, you couldn't get a slice of pizza after 8pm, you couldn't walk anywhere, and a car was a necessity, not a luxury, back in those days.

I do have to say this about Cruella—she was an animal lover. I will give her credit for that, and right after moving in, we got a female collie mix, Sheba. It was great having a dog again.

I met a great friend. My high school buddy was Justine and we had shirts that said "best friends" and our names on the back; you know, those stupid shirts with your names on them that are airbrushed. They were all the rage in the 80s. I even tried out and made the booster squad for the football team. This would be totally out of character today, but I needed to fit in and this is what teenage girls on Staten Island did—they belonged to cliques.

It's about this time when my sister Patty, who, about a year or two earlier, ventured off to California with my nieces, Melissa and Aimee, who were 7 and 5, respectively. She had to be sent for and when she returned home, her sorry excuse for a husband was drinking. He was an alcoholic and became abusive. My brother sent for her and the girls and bought them back to New York and set them up in a bungalow-type house he had purchased with two bedrooms in the South Beach section of Staten Island. This made Cruella hot.

During this time, I started to show signs of being quick-tempered and short on patience. I would do things like beat things until they broke, like curling irons if my hair didn't come out exactly perfect. If I couldn't get my homework right, I would rip paper to shreds and burn it. I had a hard time concentrating in class. My mind would wander and be off somewhere else, and things seemed to come at me quickly. It was the start of the racing thoughts—or my hypomania. I was rarely sleeping through the night and I would often cry and rock myself out of frustration over being unable to sleep. Sometimes I didn't sleep more than an hour or two a night for days. Again, I said nothing, but I felt that something was wrong, very wrong.

My brother bought a vacation home in the Pocono Mountains. While that sounds grand, it was just a double-wide trailer in a vacation mobile home park in Milford, PA, but it was sweet. We would go up there and spend weekends. I would horseback ride, and we'd bring friends and family up, and have holidays there. It was really a neat spot.

1985 arrived and I was turning Sweet 16. As my luck would have it, on the day I was supposed to have the big shindig, we got Hurricane Gloria so my friends and I all hung out in my basement and drank beer and smoked cigarettes. I was never much of a beer drinker or a smoker, but when in Rome.

This is also about the time my sister Barbara was able to patch things up with my brother. She came and saw me the day after my Sweet Sixteen and brought me a pretty pink bra and panty set—very grown-up and I loved it. I remember being excited that after all the teasing of being flat-chested from the boys, I was finally fitting into a C cup. Watch what you wish for—I am now a DDD.

Finally, all of my years of praying for Cruella's demise had been answered. My brother announced he was getting a divorce. I remember the night he asked for the divorce—said he just wasn't happy. He'd given me a heads up and I listened to him tell her so hard through my bedroom floor in the attic, I lost an earring. Pumping my fists in the air, I let out a loud "YES!" The little voice in my head said, "Now we can get back to normal, and oh, guess what, bitch? I won!"

# Part II
# Different, Very Different

*"When a Person Shows You Who
They Are Believe Them."*
—Maya Angelou

# Chapter 6
## Everything isn't Always What It Seems
## 1986

I was going into my senior year at Tottenville that September, which would have me just turning 17. I was always a good student, for the most part; my toughest subject was math, believe it or not. Go figure. Financial crime, but went to summer school for Algebra. It wasn't until my brother said math is simply money . . . now I understood.

That summer I met a boy named Larry through my friend Justine. We met at her family barbeque in July. Larry was super cool. He lived in Brooklyn, had just graduated high school, and had a job working at Roll and Roaster, a fast-food joint we all liked in Sheepshead Bay. Larry also had his own car and this is what made him the coolest of all. This would be my first summer not going to Virginia; obviously love and separation anxiety won out over that option.

Larry would pick me up take me to the movies, the mall, for ice cream and just to hang out. We were falling in love and had a great summer. The things I loved best about Larry were that he was a *man*: he was in charge and he always made me feel like he could provide for and take care of me. He bought me great gifts—teddy bears, balloons, flowers, jewelry (come on, you know you had to have an ankle bracelet with your names engraved to prove you had a boyfriend back then—well, mine was one with sapphires and diamonds). He also bought me this cool double heart ring—two hearts back-to-back with one filled with diamonds.

My brother thought Larry was a smartass punk, but he tolerated him. After all, if he had forbidden me, I would have just seen Larry behind his back. After a while, Larry grew on him and was part of the family.

Larry's mom loved me. She and his father were divorced, but still lived in the same house. His father had the apartment in the basement and dated the next-door neighbor (now tell me that's not a kick in the pants). There's no nice way to say this—Larry's father despised me. I'm not sure what bothered him more: that I wasn't Jewish or that I was part Italian. Don't get me wrong; he took us to nice places and was very cordial, but he never really warmed up to me.

I was getting my license that fall. I went to Driver's Ed and it was time to take the road test, so I opted to take it in Brooklyn rather than Staten Island. Why, you ask? Well, Larry's mother was the inspector who gave me my test. We pulled up at the location where she was working in Sheepshead Bay. She got into the car and said, "Drive around the corner. Now park. OK, you pass." That was my first introduction into the world of 'it's not what you know; it's who you know.' And I drove off with my license.

My first car was my brother's old 1977 Chevy Caprice Classic. This was not a car; it was a boat. And the passenger-side quarter panel looked like an accordion from an accident in the city with a bus . . . but who cares? It drove and I didn't have to take the bus anymore.

One of the first trips I took off of Staten Island with my new car without anyone knowing was to visit my father's grave at St. John's cemetery in Queens. Like I said earlier, we always visited my mother's; in fact, it was almost ceremony at this point. I went to the Visitors' building and asked if we they could locate Salvatore Favara. After a few minutes, the lady came back with a map and a location, and off I went. No one cared for his grave. It was overgrown with weeds and wild flowers, and looked as if it hadn't been touched in years. I remember saying, "Hello, Daddy. It's been a long time, but I'm here now." This was the first of many regular trips I took alone to visit my father and pay the same respect to him that we had to my mother all these years.

My senior year, I had enough credits to only have to take three classes, so I enrolled in the Co-Op Education Program, a program in New York City Schools enabling kids with good grades to go into a work/study program at a corporation somewhere in Manhattan. It was set up so that you worked at your job one week and went to school one week—pretty cool. I was hired at Citicorp as a clerk in HR and I loved it. I felt like a real grown-up and I had a paycheck. At this point, I was also allowed to spend weekends at Larry's house. He would pick me up from work or school on a Friday and we would hang out in Brooklyn and do couple's stuff.

Come October, it was getting colder and was flu season. I wound up with a nasty stomach flu and felt like being in my own bed, so I asked Larry to take me home on Saturday instead of Sunday. And that's when the world, as I knew it, changed. I got as far as the porch and saw my brother kissing another man on the couch through the open drapes to the living room window.

I was frozen, speechless, mortified, embarrassed, and betrayed. What fresh hell was this? Now I have never been homophobic or prejudiced. I wasn't raised that way, but this was personal. This was *me* this was happening to. I cleared my throat, fumbled for keys to the door, made loud noises so they would stop what they were doing and know I was coming. My brother never knew I saw him in the act. He just thought I surmised, and sent my sisters to have the Talk with me a few days later.

They asked if I knew and I said I suspected and that I was pissed because he was not who he said he was all these years and he had lied to me. I felt if he and I were supposed to be as close as we were, he should have told me himself.

I couldn't stand him. I didn't even want to be in the same room with him. If I was home, I locked myself in my room. The sight of him made me sick. It didn't pass for a very, very long time.

It was getting close to the holiday season and the end of 1986, and my brother just didn't look right. He was drawn and losing weight, and he was always tired. So he went to the doctor and they ran several weeks' worth of tests but couldn't come to any conclusions. He got so run-down he wound up in the hospital with pneumonia. At first they suspected Epstein Barr or some other type of auto-immune illness. Then, after three weeks in the hospital, we got the definite diagnosis—HIV-Positive. In 1986 this was a death sentence. They traced the origin of the HIV to a blood transfusion he'd had in 1978 during surgery after his arm accident during our first move. I'm sure that being in the closet for so many years and having unprotected sex didn't help the situation either.

I felt like a complete asshole. Here I was, feeling sorry for myself because I had been lied to, and my brother was going to die. I did what I always did when hit with devastating, life-altering news—I sucked it up and I panicked. I realized in a split instant that his diagnosis meant that the only parent I had ever known was going to die and I was going to be left alone again.

# CHAPTER 7
# HOUSTON . . . WE HAVE A
# PROBLEM!
# 1987

**M**y brother left his position at the Village Nursing Home and tried to simplify his life, going on medical leave when he came home from the hospital. He decided that it was hard enough taking care of himself, so I should go live with my sister Patty in a house he purchased on Graham Avenue in the Bulls Head section of Staten Island.

After the holidays, I packed my stuff and went to live with Patty. This was an awkward move, as there was really no room for me there. Melissa and Aimee each had a room, and, well, my white bedroom set and I were shit out of luck. But my sister, always one to help, let me have Melissa's room, while Melissa and Aimee shared Aimee's room.

My best buddy Justine came by to visit me in my new place and our next-door neighbors happened to be outside when Justine's mom dropped her off. Little did we know that Justine's mom was having a long-standing affair with the father of the girl next door. Justine never knew. Now she did, and so did her father. Needless to say, it was an ugly mess and that was her last time visiting me there. What were the odds of that?

My guess is this put us right around February and I finally went to my sister's for the "Talk." I told them that Larry and I were ready to have sex and could they help me get birth control? Barbara took me to the local Family Planning Clinic on Staten Island and got me my very first prescription for birth control pills. The doctor said to give it one full month before having sex without a condom, so we did. The big night came and Larry took me to his bedroom and we made love, and you would think that I would have been ecstatic. But in all reality, I was disappointed and I said, "Is that it? Is that what I have been worried about all this time?" He said, "Yep, that's it, but you'll like it more after you've done it a few more times." There, right there. Truer words have never been spoken.

I was going to school and work and staying with Larry on weekends and spending a couple of nights back in Annadale with my brother. Things were not okay between us; there was still a lot of tension and now he had a "boyfriend" so I was just a little uncomfortable. I simply just didn't know how to act.

I passed my SAT with a 2,340 and I could have opted for a scholarship somewhere, but after graduation, I decided I would work full-time. I loved working, I loved making money. Citicorp offered me a full-time position making $20,000 a year as a secretary to the head of their legal counsel division at the corporate level, so off I went to the headquarters at 399 Park Avenue and reported to my boss. She was a wonderful lady. I was extremely lucky to have such a generous, caring individual for a boss, who took her time with me and showed me the ropes.

I had a full benefits package and there was a tuition reimbursement program. I started taking classes at night at Pace University, which was right in downtown Manhattan.

I was making the schlep, and that is what it was—a schlep from Staten Island to Manhattan every day. I lived too far out on the Island, which made the ferry inconvenient, so I took an express bus.

Now that I had medical insurance, I began to make inquiries and phone calls to therapists on Staten Island because, let's face it, this was long overdue. I found a therapist in Village Greens, a subdivision in the Arden Heights section of Staten Island, which, if I took the local bus, was on my way to the express bus. So once a week, the night I stayed at my brother's, I stopped in for an hour-long session in the morning with Donna Johnson. After the first month of sessions, she referred me to a psychiatrist, Dr. Ryan at Staten Island University Hospital, who did an "intake" and told me that, after filling out a half-hour's worth of questions about my childhood, I was manic depressive (it wasn't really called bipolar yet). When I heard the diagnosis, I said, "How is that possible?" He said, "It's simple, really. You were predisposed genetically, and the trauma of losing both your parents in such a short period of time, coupled with the difficulty you're having accepting your brother's sexual preference and medical condition, flipped your genetic switch to the 'on' position."

I remember two things about this meeting: one, I thought he was a quack, and two, I thought he was a quack and knew nothing about me and what was wrong with me. How could he possibly know by answering those questions and talking to me for five minutes that I was crazy? He gave me a 30-day prescription for Lithium, Prozac and Ativan and told me to continue seeing Donna, my therapist. I got outside his office and I threw the prescription in the first garbage can I saw, and that ended my therapy and the thought of returning back to see the quack.

Larry and I decided to get our own apartment after my 18th birthday in September, and we moved to a little one-bedroom basement apartment in the Marine Park Section of Brooklyn near 36th Street and Avenue S. It was a great spot—$600/month for rent and right across the street from the bus stop, which took me to the D train at the 16th Street Station in Sheepshead Bay. It was about an hour-long commute to 399 Park. Most of the time, Larry picked me up at night because of school. At this point, Larry was working as a repo man for a bank, repossessing cars from people that reneged on loans. Dangerous job, but he loved it. I went with him once on a weekend and we got shot at, so I thought, 'I've seen enough, you're on your own.'

Larry and I didn't have much, but we both worked and made decent money. We had a furnished apartment, a car (a 1984 Chrysler New Yorker), and a full fridge. We were big on eating out, and we did lots of that. These were happy times.

I made my brother dinner in our new apartment. It was the first time I did the entertaining and he was proud—I was living on my own, had a nice place and was a good hostess. He felt he had done something right in raising me. That evening, after coffee and dessert, he gave me my parents' jewelry that he had been saving for me. He thought now was the time to give it to me, so I inherited my father's pinkie ring and medal and chain and my mother's diamond cocktail ring, a sergeant ring, a charm bracelet and two pairs of earnings—one diamond and one emerald. I was really touched when he gave them to me. This was all I had left of my parents and I treasured them.

Living with Larry made me feel safe and wanted, and that was the best feeling. Screw what that doctor said. It would pass; it was just a matter of time.

# CHAPTER 8
# IT SOUNDED LIKE A GOOD
# IDEA
# 1988–1989

I was in the Staten Island Mall and walked by a furniture store and said to Larry, "That looks like my brother, Bobby," and it was. I went up to him to say hi. Now, the last time I saw him, he was at my sister Barbara's wedding in the mid-70s, but he recognized me right away. It was awkward, but we made plans for me to go to his house on Staten Island and have dinner. I felt like I was walking on the moon. This was just fantastic; I was going to be reunited with my long-lost brother. My first instinct was don't tell Ricky, but I did and he encouraged me to get to know him. And we visited on and off for a couple years. At one point, Larry even got a job working for him at the Key Food warehouse in Brooklyn. But we never really developed a relationship. Disappointing, really. It would have been nice to have him in my life.

My sister Patty had a male friend named Pat, who had a Porsche 954, red with black interior. He wanted his car to disappear so he could report it stolen and collect the insurance money on it. The two of them went to Larry, who, by this point, had a reputation for being a little—how shall we say this—crooked. Pat and Larry agreed the car would disappear. Well . . . that's not what happened. What happened was Larry took the car to a chop shop, had the VIN numbers changed, and kept it for himself. Pat didn't know. Larry went through with his plan and Pat was none the wiser.

We had the car for about a month when Larry said, "Hey, let's do the same thing Pat did. Let's get rid of the car, report it stolen, and keep the insurance money." I want to say the value of the car in those days was about $40,000 or so. I thought, 'You know what? This doesn't sound half bad, and we could do a lot with that money. Okay, I'm in. What do I have to do?'

The cars were registered and insured to me, but we used my sister Debbie's address in Long Island, which was in Suffolk County because the rates were cheaper. Of course, being the criminal that I am today, this makes no sense. He had us go to the Green Acres Mall in Valley Stream on Long Island because he didn't want the car to be out of the insurance coverage area, when in fact the mall was in Nassau County and not Suffolk. That doesn't make sense today, but what did I know at the time? He was the mastermind at this point, not me. We reported the car stolen from there.

The police officer at the mall took our information, and we hung around a little pretending to look for it and seem distraught, and about an hour later, we left. Have you figured out what's wrong with our story? One, we had a car there to leave in, and two, the mall was under surveillance and they never saw us come onto the property in a Porsche, just the New Yorker. Ha! Gotcha.

We were about 15 minutes away from the mall on the LIE when we heard the sirens, and an undercover car pulled us over and told us we were being taken in for questioning.

They separated us. They said he was telling on me and they told him I was telling on him. Neither was true and we were both street-smart enough to know it. The only thing that saved us from being held over was that we were clean-cut and white. We were booked for a Class 6D Felony of Insurance Fraud. Oh, boy, how was I going to explain this?

I had to find a lawyer. I knew even then, if you don't have someone good, you're going down. We told my sister Patty, who was furious. After that wore off, she asked a detective friend of hers at the time whom we should talk to, and he sent us to an attorney named Dennis J. Peterson. Great guy—sketches of a famous mob trial on the walls, and charged us $4,000 ($2,000 each). But he bargained us down to a misdemeanor, falsifying a police report with no probation because we were first-time offenders.

I remember the day we were sentenced. The Judge said to me, "I want to give you some advice, young lady. Get yourself some help and get rid of him," as he pointed to Larry. Clairvoyant, actually, in retrospect.

Larry and I got engaged and made things more official that year, with the ring and the party and the whole nine yards. A nice rock, I might add; a one-carat solitaire in a channel setting. Classy. I invited my brother Bobby and his family. He was a no-show. I was pissed already, besides the fact that he'd promised and I'd paid for five dinners that didn't get eaten. Then the most embarrassing moment of my life happened—there was a slow song. I want to say it was "Always & Forever" by Heatwave or something sappy like that. I had my back to the dance floor and I was talking to Larry. He said, "You'd better turn around," and that's when I saw it. My brother was slow dancing with his boyfriend, also named Rick. Big Dick and Little Dick was how I referred to them. No one except my family knew he was gay; I kept it a secret. All of our friends and Larry's family laughed and snickered and pointed and I just hung my head and turned every shade of red. I was humiliated. Two things were certain by the end of the night: both my brothers sucked and my secret was out.

1989 was the last year I went to Virginia. Larry and I went as a couple for Loretta's wedding in July and then a couple of times after that, but things were so unsettled for me in my own mind with my brother and the whole gay thing and work and school that I convinced myself I just didn't have the time to go anymore. In all actuality, it was the beginning of my paranoia. If I leave, everything will fall apart. If I go, everything will be gone when I get back.

Later that year, my brother came to Larry and me and said he was strapped financially, due to the cost of his treatment, and even though he had just returned to full-time work at Clove Lakes Nursing Home in Staten Island, he was struggling and wanted to get out from under the house payment on Graham Avenue, to downsize and buy a small townhouse for him and his boyfriend in the Rosebank section of Staten Island. He asked Larry and me if we would do him the favor and buy the house because the market was bad and looking for a buyer may take a while. We kicked it around. Honestly, I hated that house, but Larry thought it was a great opportunity to own something. When I asked him where Patty would go, he said that he had done enough and she would just have to move and he would talk to her—for me not to worry about it. He would take care of handling Patty.

The purchase of this house that I hated, especially because I did not care for the neighbors, is still a point of contention between me and Patty today. I thought I was helping and I never intended to make her life more difficult. My brother didn't so much as help her get her apartment and get moved. At this point, we started to see the true pent-up feelings of resentment about taking care of us his whole life start to surface.

Larry and I moved to Graham Avenue, but it was short-lived. I hated it there. We were at the point in our relationship where we were becoming strangers. We wanted different things—he wanted a family, and I wasn't ready. He wanted a wife to stay home and cook and clean, and I was maturing and growing more and more independent. I was interested in my career and school. I had just been accepted into the part-time MBA program at Stern and I had high hopes of becoming successful.

It wasn't more than six months before the pressures of the mortgage (roughly $1,700) and the credit card bills started to wear on us and we drifted further and further apart. It was my birthday (1989) and I decided I was going to get a tattoo. Now, back in these days, these were outlawed in New York City so Patty took me to a place in New Jersey and I got my first of 21 tattoos that night, and it made Larry furious that I would mark my body like that. I had it done on my upper right thigh. It was Betty Boop giving a moon, and I said, "Get over it, Larry—my leg is going to be around a lot longer than you."

By December of that year, the use of drugs, stealing from his job that my brother got him at Key Food, loan sharking to his co-workers, and the cheating were more than I wanted to bear anymore. Larry had become like his father, someone he said he would never be—hurtful, demeaning and controlling. And one day I had enough. I called work one morning and said I was sick. I was sick, sick and tired. Told my boss I wouldn't be in and I packed my bags and I left. I moved into Patty's apartment and didn't look back.

Larry begged and pleaded with me to come home. He brought me flowers, and for a split second, I considered. But I knew if I went back to him, I would have to be willing to be nothing more than a housewife with a baby on each hip, barefoot and pregnant, serving him dinner after he got home from just screwing his girlfriend. And for once, I took a stand and put my foot down with him and said, "NO!"

A month later, I found out I was pregnant. I couldn't figure out how. I was being so careful. I never thought about telling him for one second. I went to the Family Planning Clinic in Manhattan on a Friday and had an abortion. I remember feeling guilty and like a horrible person, but I wasn't ready to be a mom and I didn't want to be stuck with him for the rest of my life.

# Chapter 9
## The Rebound
### 1990–1991

I didn't stay at Patty's long—a month, tops. If finding out my brother was gay wasn't disturbing enough, this next piece of information put the icing on the cake. Patty let me know that she met someone—a woman—and that they would be moving in together, so now my brother and my sister were gay. But somehow the news of Patty's being gay wasn't as shocking and disturbing as that of my brother. Maybe it was simply because I didn't love her the way I loved my brother, which was more like a parent than a sibling. I accepted it.

I found a little studio-type condo I could rent on Richmond Hill Road behind the Staten Island Mall. When I left Larry, I literally left with just my clothes. When I moved into my apartment, I slept on the floor the first week. By that weekend, I had a sectional sofa bed couch, a coffee table, two end tables, an entertainment center (all white lacquer, of course), a glass kitchen table and four chairs, a TV, lamps and kitchen stuff.

For a housewarming present, my brother gave me a cat. It was his cat, except with the medication he was taking, he became highly allergic. So I inherited Mimi. He said she would be good company and she was.

This was a great location since I didn't have a car. I could walk down the street and jump on the bus to work or walk over to the mall if I wanted to get out for a bit. And so I was single. This was completely new territory. I had always lived with someone—my mom, my brother, my sister, Larry. Now it was just me and I was scared.

At this point, I had gone from losing just a couple hours of sleep a night to full-on manic episodes. I would stay up three days at a time and not feel the need to rest. It made it great to get through work and college. Don't get me wrong, but that little voice inside my head kept saying you know this isn't right. Normal people can close their eyes and go to sleep at night. I knew it wasn't insomnia. I knew in my heart the diagnosis by Dr. Ryan two years prior was correct, but I wouldn't allow myself to accept that I was mentally ill. If this were true, then I was weak and fatally flawed.

I was anxious to play the field . . . you know, sow my oats. So I started sleeping with my bus driver. This was, to date, the second man I'd slept with. Larry had been my one and only. And my sisters were right. You don't know how bad the sex you're having is until you have something to compare it to. And the sex I was having with the bus driver was outstanding! I couldn't have been sleeping with the bus driver for more than a couple of weeks when I ran into my neighbor from across the hall. A good-looking guy—well-built, pretty eyes, hazel. I would get flustered when he'd start a conversation. We would either meet waiting for the elevator or taking the trash to the incinerator. He asked what I did and I told him I was working at Kidder Peabody on Wall Street in the Investment Banking department as an assistant learning the ropes on how to do an IPO (take a company public), and that I was one year away from finishing the MBA program at Stern. I asked what he did, and there was a long pause . . . he said, "Well, I'm retired." I said, "Yeah, right." He wasn't more than 30. He said, "Nah, I got laid off from the Exchange (he was a stock broker) and now I deal drugs." And I laughed. He said, "No, seriously, I deal coke around here." And then I was quiet. Then I asked, "Do you want to come over for dinner? I can make you some pasta and we can watch a movie or something," and he said, "Sure, that sounds like fun." He said he would bring the drinks and we set up for Friday that week. Now, seriously, a normal person would have run the other direction. I found his choice of career fascinating.

Friday night arrived and I made Chicken Angelo, which is chicken breast with white wine, garlic and artichokes. I had red potatoes with peas and rosemary and I made stuffed mushrooms for an appetizer and cheesecake for dessert (still a signature dessert of mine today). Darryl brought over a fifth of Absolut and some grapefruit juice and we made Greyhounds. We drank the whole bottle. We were drunk and, finally, the clothes came off and there we were on my coffee table getting down and dirty.

It went on like this for weeks—every chance we got, we had sex. Then one night he said he was wondering if I wouldn't mind if a few of our now mutual friends came up to my apartment, since I had nice furniture and he didn't. I said sure and he said, "We are going to do a little partying. We all party on the weekends . . . you don't mind, do you?" By partying, he meant do coke. I said sure, no problem, it will be fun. Our friends Kim and Tony came by and we all sat around listening to old school disco and reminiscing about clubs and stuff we did in Brooklyn. Then they started to line the coke up on my glass table and I asked if I could try it. This was the first drug I ever tried. I was 21 and I thought, hell, what's the worst thing that could happen?

I loved it. Not only did I enjoy the high, but you could drink to your heart's content and not be drunk, and everyone with you was also wide awake and the fact that I wasn't sleeping didn't matter—I had company. And that is how we spent our weekends from Friday night sundown to Sunday morning sunrise: we partied. We had two rules. One is we only partied on weekends and holidays, and two, we only partied with his profits, not his supply. If you believe we kept those two commandments, I have some swamp land in Florida I would like to sell you.

Larry was still in touch and he couldn't keep his head above water. He was losing everything and going bankrupt, and told me if I didn't take over the house on Graham Avenue, it was going to be foreclosed on and since it was in both our names, my credit would suffer. I talked to Darryl and at this point, we were together for a few months, basically living in one apartment, so we talked and agreed to move into the house and take over the payments. We both packed up our apartment and headed over to Graham Avenue. Did I mention I hated this house and the neighbors? Oh, I did . . . but what could I do? I was stuck. I hated every minute of being back in that house.

We celebrated the holidays and then Darryl got the call from his mom in Las Vegas. His dad was diabetic and deteriorating rapidly and Darryl needed to go be with his father. I was graduating from Stern in May so we talked and decided that I would sell the house and we both would move to Las Vegas. At this point, I had only been to Vegas once with him to meet his parents, but I didn't want him to go without me and he was very persuasive and promised me a house and car. So I went.

We put Graham Avenue up for sale in January of 1991 and didn't get any bites. I finally just let it go; it was an albatross. It bankrupted me—the mortgage, along with my credit cards and student loans, were killing me. Honestly, if filing bankruptcy was the answer to getting rid of the horrible house, I was doing it. I went bankrupt at 22.

I'm not sure why my sisters all sided with Patty, but even I felt I did her dirty on taking over Graham Avenue. And I don't want to say at this point they were totally against me, but there was an underlying unhappiness with the way things went down. If they only knew I did it to help my brother because he asked, never because I wanted to. My brother was involved in his new life with his new boyfriend and new friends, and being gay to him was a novelty. Maybe I too would have felt the same if I pretended to be somebody I wasn't my entire life, but he was no longer in the parental role I'd once held for him; he was demoted to just another person who deserted me and left me heartbroken. The Ricky that I knew and loved was gone.

It was May and I received my diploma from Stern. I decided not to go to graduation because it meant that I would have to take off of work, which was my only escape, and between me, you and the fence post, nobody knew I got my degree. Honestly, I was a great student (3.6 GPA) but my family was so wrapped up in the own drama of their own lives and I was so coked out most of the time or manic that I didn't believe anyone would care or would be genuinely impressed or happy for me. I just picked it up in the Dean's office and threw it in a drawer next to my Bachelor's from Pace.

I told my brother we would be leaving for Vegas in June and he didn't take too kindly to that. Of course, it wasn't because he would miss me, with all his new friends and new life. He just didn't feel Darryl and I were together long enough for a move like that. But guess what? This was my chance (if ever I was going to get one) to get out, a chance to start over, and a new life in a new city on the opposite side of the country. I was taking it. This meant no more dealing with his gay shit, no more Larry, no more bills, no more commute to Wall Street. This meant I may start to feel normal. This meant I was free.

# Part III
# The Move West

*"IT'S BETTER TO LIVE YOUR OWN DESTINY IMPERFECTLY THAN TO LIVE AN IMITATION OF SOMEBODY ELSE'S LIFE WITH PERFECTION."*
—*BHAGAVAD GITA*

# CHAPTER 10
# DOROTHY, YOU'RE NOT IN KANSAS ANYMORE
# 1991–1992

W e drove, and took three weeks to get to Vegas and stopped in every major city along Route 66. We had a great time. Of course, I still had Mimi and we flew her out ahead of time and Darryl's parents kept her at their house while we made the trip.

The first year in Vegas was interesting. Vegas was just starting to develop—the mega resort was making its debut and the newest hotel on the strip was the Mirage. I was convinced I would never get used to it. I cried for New York. I was sure I made the wrong decision by moving. I was homesick.

We moved into a one-bedroom apartment in the Village Green complex in Henderson just north of Green Valley. We got a puppy, a pit bull we named Shana. Work was scarce and really, the only way to get into a casino was if you knew someone, so I took a job as a secretary for a trash company, Silver State Disposal, at their recycling facility in North Las Vegas, which was about a half-hour drive door to door.

On my first day, I met my new boss and I fell in instant lust with him. The attraction was mutual. The voice of reason was saying 'don't shit where you eat' but my hormones were in overdrive. After several weeks of playing cat and mouse, I had my first official affair. Darryl and weren't married but I was cheating. And I was enjoying it.

At this point, I already knew Darryl was cheating on me. No one in particular—just anything that walked. He was a player. He was now dealing meth; coke was too expensive on the West Coast and shipping it FedEx, which he had done on a couple of occasions, was extremely dangerous so he changed his product line and had a supplier in a real seedy section of downtown.

I was working for Silver State for about a year and we were now into the middle of 1992. I was still having an affair with my boss when the worst thing possible happened: I got pregnant. Not by choice or stupidity but by sheer accident. I was taking antibiotics for a cut on my leg that got infected and it counteracted my birth control and made me fertile. Of course Darryl had no idea I was cheating and at this point, not only with my boss. I also had an affair going with one of the drivers. I am positive the baby was not Darryl's; we just weren't having regular sex. But I wasn't 100% sure whose it was, so I told Darryl it was his. Darryl wanted the baby and I said, "Absolutely not," that I wasn't ready, when really, in the back of my mind, I was afraid it would turn out to be mentally ill like me. He understood and respected my decision—he wasn't too thrilled about it either. We found a private doctor, Dr. Ames, and I had an abortion. I knew at this point I would never have children. It's not to say I am not motherly, I just had no desire down deep in my soul. I think the fear of having a child and possibly passing off genetically what I considered a curse was the deal breaker for me.

I knew it was time to end the affair and start looking for a new job. I kept my ear to the ground and I went to a staffing agency and gave them my resume, which had my education listed on it. The lady at the staffing agency, Joyce, told me if you want a job in this town, you better dummy it down. I said, "What do you mean?" She said, "Most people won't want to hire someone smarter than them." We took it off. A couple weeks later, she called and told me that she had a client, MGM Grand, Inc. (the corporate office, not the hotel), and they needed an administrative assistant for one of their senior executives and she thought I would be perfect. I went on the interview and thought I was impressive. I showed up in my black Wall Street suit with a leather portfolio with recommendation letters and my resume. My future boss, being as he was skeptical of everyone, needed some time to think about it and wanted to finish interviewing a couple of candidates they had already scheduled and told me to call him directly on Wednesday and he would give me answer. But before he ended the interview, he said, "I am going to ask you a question that's against the law." I said, "Okay . . ." He said, "How old are you?" I said, "I am 23." He said, "I'm sorry—you said 23?" I said, "Yes," and he said, "You're not 32?" I said, "No, I'm pretty sure I'm 23," and he said, "Okay, I will talk to you on Wednesday." By Vegas standards, this was a great job—$35,000 a year, full benefits, and I would be working for one of the most notable businessmen in the city, not to mention he reported to one of the most successful businessmen in the world.

Wednesday arrived and I couldn't contain myself. I gave it till after lunch and I called. He was unavailable. I immediately counted myself out; he was avoiding me so he didn't have to give me the bad news. Then a couple of hours later, my phone rang and it was him. I called him by his last name and thanked him for returning my call, and he asked, "When are you going to start calling your new boss by his first name?" and I said, "Okay, I can do that, Boss."

# CHAPTER 11
# THE DUTCH GIRL WITH THE
# FINGER IN THE DAM
# 1993

I was working at MGM about a year. I had long since quit the partying with the cocaine and meth and was taking my position and my new career very seriously. There was no taking any chances—I was in the big time and I knew it. One night my boss and I left the office together, and he said, "Let me walk you to your car." I said, "No, it's okay—it's just right there," and I pointed just a few spaces down from his. He said, "That is not a car, Chris; that is a hideous *excuse* for a car." I was driving Darryl's 1985 Pontiac Grand Prix, which, with limo tinted windows and pin striping, looked like a real drug dealer's car. I said, "Well, it gets me from point A to B." He said, "Tomorrow, get a ride to my house and I will give you my extra car. You can't be seen driving that thing if you work for me." The next morning I drove to his house in the Lakes and he handed me the keys to his 1987 Mercedes 560SL. I wasn't sure what to do—I didn't know how to drive a stick, so I just sat it in it and stared at the steering wheel. He said, "What's wrong?" I said, "I can't drive a stick," and he said, "It's an automatic." I said, "That looks like a stick shift." He said, "Yes, it's intentionally designed that way." It was the first of many extravagant gifts from my boss.

Well, the time has come; I'm finally going to crack. You were waiting for this, weren't you? I was travelling with my boss in Los Angeles. He was giving an investor speech that evening, and he was the keynote speaker at a gaming industry conference. We were spending the night and heading out early in the morning. One of the perks of MGM was we flew on private aircraft; we could set our own schedule. I was in a hotel room that evening when I got my first panic attack before dinner. I thought I was having a heart attack. I managed to talk myself down and get myself to the dinner and work the slide presentation, but right after he delivered his speech, I excused myself and went to my room. I couldn't sleep, as usual, and stayed up that night and watched TV and tossed and turned like I always had, trying to see if I could find a comfortable position and just pass out. In the morning, fear and paranoia and the dreaded terrors had taken over and I couldn't leave my hotel room—I was paralyzed. On top of that, I was panicking because we were to meet in the lobby in less than an hour to head back to Vegas. But I couldn't talk myself out of it this time. I swallowed my pride and I called my boss and told him I wasn't feeling well and could we leave a little later? He said sure and asked if another hour would help. It didn't. When I wasn't down in the lobby before him, which was my usual M.O. (to be early and never keep him waiting), he came to my room. When he took a look at me, he knew there was something drastically wrong. He asked if he could come in and he saw breakfast from room service was untouched. He asked if it was the flu or a virus or if I had just been working too hard and I don't know what it was about him, but I knew I could trust him. He already had trusted me with so much and I said, "I think I need to talk," and he sat in the chair at the table and listened. I dumped on him everything that had happened to me in my life thus far and told him I thought the doctor in Staten Island was right—that I was mentally ill. He looked at me straight-faced and said, "You're a valuable employee and I can't afford to have you institutionalized." Always about him. "You need help. Let's get back to Vegas and I will get you some help."

My boss was true to his word: he set me up with an appointment with a private doctor, and what wasn't paid for by my insurance was covered by him. I met with Dr. Laborati, who then in turn recommended a therapist, Sue Daniel. I went to talk therapy once a week and I went to have my prescriptions checked once a month. Dr. Laborati stood by the diagnosis rendered in 1987 by Dr. Ryan and agreed with his choice of medication and put me on some regimen of Lithium, Prozac and Ativan.

Dr. Laborati and Sue Daniel recommended that I start doing some reading and educating myself about the disease. They suggested *An Unquiet Mind* by Dr. Kay Redfield Jamison, who, in my opinion, is the foremost authority on Bipolar Disorder, and then they suggested the *Feeling Good Handbook* by David D. Burns. It was comforting to know I wasn't alone and to hear someone else describe the paranoia, racing thoughts, hypomania, sleeplessness, panic and promiscuity. I felt Dr. Redfield Jamison was reading my mind. It somehow gave me peace. I also thought it was pretty cool that I would be classified as being Manic Depressive with the likes of Mozart, Van Gogh and Churchill. I was keeping pretty good company.

In May, Darryl and I bought and moved into our first home on Luanda Avenue in the Longford Homes subdivision of Annie Oakley Street in Las Vegas. We added two more dogs to our family: a Chihuahua named Trixie and a German Shepherd/Doberman mix named Buster. It was a cute, little three-bedroom home on a nice half-acre lot. On June 7th, Darryl and I married. Why? To this day, I don't know—partly because I wanted to seem stable and I know he wanted his father to see at least one of his sons get married before he died. We had a nice wedding in the Desert Inn Hotel and a Sunday brunch. We flew my brother in to give me away, and my sisters Debbie and Barbara came with him. They were more excited about coming to Vegas than they were about the wedding. My boss was nice enough to put them up at the Desert Inn. We had a Jewish ceremony out of respect for Darryl's parents. It was really quite lovely.

The medication seemed to be working, I really did feel good and I was enjoying therapy—it felt good to just get everything off my chest. I genuinely liked my doctors and I felt, for the first time, I was making progress. However, I was unhappy with the side effects of the medications. I was steadily gaining weight and by the fall of 1993, I had gone from a size 8 to a size 14. I hated to look at myself in the mirror. I was depressed about it so I decided to join Jenny Craig. That worked: I was back down to an 8 by the time we had grand opening of the MGM Grand Hotel in December. I vowed never to put on another pound and stopped taking my medication for vanity's sake. I never told my boss or my doctors I stopped the medication. I would get the prescriptions, refill them and throw them in the trash. I felt fine; they'd done their job. I'm better now. I feel great, I look great. I'm cured.

# CHAPTER 12
# THIRD TIME'S A CHARM
# 1994

I liken my years spent at MGM to dog years: one year equaled seven. I put in a lot of hours. By the time New Years Eve of 1994 rolled around, I had walking pneumonia and was banished by everyone to a hotel room until I felt better. The doctor was called and put me on antibiotics and ordered bed rest for a week.

A month later I was pregnant again—can you believe this? The antibiotics counteracted my birth control again. I mean, seriously, what are the odds? This was most inconvenient, as my career had taken off. I didn't have time to be sick or down so I scheduled an abortion with Dr. Ames and in the same procedure, he gave me a tubal ligation. I removed all chances from this horrible choice having to be made ever again. I not only had the tubes tied; I had them cauterized. Permanent and irreversible. I was 24.

Spring had arrived and Darryl decided to get a real job—said he was bored and quitting the drug business. He got a job as a bus driver for Citizens Area Transit, which was short-lived. He said he couldn't handle dealing with the customers, and asked me to help get him a job at MGM. I went to my boss and we were able to get him a job as a bellman at the hotel. Now it may not sound it to you, but being a bellman is a good job in

Vegas. You can easily make a hundred a night in tips, and of course, back then, that was tax-free. He liked it, but everyone knew he was married to me, so he got special treatment from the supervisors and the guys he worked with just gave him shit.

I decided the house on Luanda was too small. I wanted something bigger. This was the start of my grandiose thinking, as I was surrounded by wealth and fame and I was trying to do my best to get there myself. I talked Darryl into putting a tenant in the Luanda house and buying something bigger just across Pecos Road from Wayne Newton on Happy Circle. It was a nice half-acre lot with a ranch house with four bedrooms, four bathrooms, and lots of extras.

It was my birthday and I took the day off. I had several flower deliveries that day so I kept running to the door. This particular time, I was served a civil judgment—they were taking Darryl to court. Apparently, when he was driving the bus, he had a regular customer, a woman he would drive to the door. They would have sex on the bus then he would take her home. Well, she found out he was married, and then she found out we had assets, and she sued him. That night, he was arrested at the hotel for kidnapping and sexual assault.

I called the only person I knew who could help—my boss—and he in turn called the only person he knew could help, Oscar Goodman (now former Mayor of Las Vegas, then a known mob attorney). We bailed him out and went to Oscar's office the next day. It was palatial. He had a chandelier hanging over his desk, and Oscar told him, "Don't worry— $5,000 and this goes away. We'll get you out of it," and a month later, he was good to his word. Darryl was convicted of a misdemeanor (open and gross lewdness) and asked to attend drug counseling.

Needless to say, he never returned to work at MGM. I was humiliated and he couldn't face the ridicule from his co-workers. He was back to his usual tricks, dealing and getting high. He was severely depressed, his father was barely hanging on, he had no job, he was plowing through his savings, he was getting high more than he was dealing, and he was simply just not happy.

I continued with treatment. I didn't take my medication but I was so involved in work that that was my drug. My life was MGM; everything I did was centered on my career. I was treated well, I was making great money, I was promoted, I had stock options, and I went from wearing Jaclyn Smith to Kmart to Gucci. I had complete autonomy. I could go wherever I wanted in town to eat, to drink, to gamble, and if I went to shows, I had the best seats. I never waited in line. I was respected. I was a VIP. My family visited often during my years at MGM, and I was always able to be a good hostess. I would get them free rooms and show or special event tickets or take them to a nice lunch or fancy dinner. My ego was enormous and I was on top of the world.

# CHAPTER 13
# PILLOW TALK WILL GET YOU
# EVERY TIME
# 1995

L iving on Happy Circle, or should I say Unhappy Circle, was frustrating. We bought the money pit. Everything that could go wrong with a house did go wrong. We made a mistake, and we were at the point where we were deciding on buying a new septic system or selling and we opted to sell. We took a bath but it was for the best. Our tenants were still in our Luanda house and that was an ideal rental property, so we bought a beautiful home on 15th Street in an older section of Las Vegas, where the homes and the landscaping were more mature. We bought a house with a lot of bells and whistles: an in-ground pool, guest cottage, circular drive, fireplace, sauna in the master bathroom. Definitely, to date, the nicest place we ever lived in or owned.

Things started to become interesting at work. My boss was in the middle of working on a top secret project for his boss, and I was working on press releases and SEC filings for the announcement. It was the announcement that Kirk Kerkorian would intend to increase his position in Chrysler Corporation. I took phone calls at home and worked odd hours and weekends, which wasn't so unusual, but Darryl was more interested in what I was doing than usual and would pump me for information and do his best to listen in on phone calls. Let's face it—he had no life, so he became obsessed with mine.

In April of 1995, we issued the press release that shook Wall Street and created pandemonium in both Chrysler's and MGM's stocks. Investors, the Street, and people who were long-time followers of Kerkorian were buying at a feverish pace, forcing stock prices to climb. It was quite a rush. Here I was, a kid from Brooklyn, on the inside of a major historical moment on Wall Street.

The dust settled and it was a few weeks after the press release when my boss called me to his office. I literally sat right outside his door. And he said, "Take a seat." I knew it was serious; usually he just spouted orders off. He said, "The SEC contacted us and Darryl traded options (options, if you had inside information, would be more lucrative than stock because you were betting that the stock would increase) the day we did the press release on Chrysler." My mouth fell open. I couldn't believe it—I was in complete and totally shock. He said, "By your expression and reaction, I can see this is a complete surprise. Did you know anything about this?" I said, "Of course not," and then I became furious. My first impulse was to go home and kill Darryl.

My boss, ever my biggest supporter, believed me and told me that he and the company and Mr. Kerkorian would stand behind me and pay for whatever legal representation I needed. I was being indemnified by the Corporation, the SEC was going to question me, and this had to be handled delicately.

I went home and into a rage and told Darryl it was over. I said I'd had enough and that if my boss and I didn't have the relationship that we did, he would have fired me and that would have been the end of my career. I told him to talk to the tenants and buy them out of the lease and start getting use to the idea he would be on his own and moving back to Luanda by himself. I wanted a divorce; this was the last straw. If he was going to kill himself, he would do it alone and not take me with him.

That June, my brother was turning 40 and this was the one and only time I flew home (during my years at MGM) for his birthday party. He wanted a big celebration so we had a big affair. DJ, buffet, you name it. I paid and I spared no expense. My sisters were nice enough to send formal invitations and inadvertently left my name off. Boy, was I ticked. But it was about my brother and I was happy to do it. It was really nice to see my family; it was the first time we were all in the same room since I don't know when. I flew back the next morning. I stayed at the Ritz Carlton that night and I remember lying in my bed thinking 'Boy, it would be nice if I could just fall asleep like a normal person.'

November of 1995 I received my subpoena. They requested the honor of my presence at their offices in Washington, DC. I couldn't refuse.

My attorney, Joe Goldstein from Crowell & Moring, prepped me for a week. He asked tough questions. Sometimes things would get heated and he would back off. The evening before my flight, my boss said to me, "This is more about Kirk than it is about you. Remember that."

I went to DC, stayed at the JW Marriot and checked in and stayed up all night and went over my testimony in my head. The next morning, we met for breakfast but I was sick to my stomach and couldn't eat. I was beyond nervous. We got the SEC building and I was intimidated by the huge seal on the marble in the lobby. I thought I was going to vomit. We got to the deposition room and it was full. Andrew Sporkin was the lead agent and then there were his assistant and a court reporter and a couple of clerks, me and my attorney. It started as all depositions do, with them asking to state and confirm your name and address, and when we got to the third or fourth question, when they asked how often Darryl and I had pillow talk, I broke down and my attorney had to call a recess. My nerves and the intimidation got the best of me, and he pulled me into a small conference room off to the side and told me to go into the ladies' room and pull myself together. He prepped me and I was prepared. I went in the bathroom, threw cold water on my face, came out and underwent four hours of questioning. We took a lunch break and then I underwent another four hours of questioning. It was a long day and then it was over. I was told I did a good job, and that I might want to consider a career as an expert witness.

I was on the plane on my way back to Las Vegas and I kept thinking how much I dreaded going back. I couldn't stand the sight of Darryl. But now that I had the deposition behind me, I could concentrate on getting rid of him as soon as possible. I called an attorney that worked in Oscar Goodman's firm, Anne Zimmerman, from the plane and made an appointment for the next evening to discuss filing for divorce; I was done and needed to move on.

# CHAPTER 14
# WITH FRIENDS LIKE THESE,
# YOU DON'T NEED ENEMIES
# 1996

I served Darryl with divorce papers in January, and he was being difficult. We agreed to split everything 50/50 with the exception of my stock options. He would get Luanda and I would get 15th Street in lieu of my stock options. He got whatever cash was in the bank (my guess is about $25,000) and the furniture.

He would say he was moving out but he never left. Finally, I called for backup and flew my brother out to help provide incentive. My brother and I checked in at the hotel and I stayed there until he and Darryl had all of Darryl's stuff moved back into Luanda Avenue. Darryl and I talked—he said he wanted to have visitation to the dogs. I agreed and I said that I was okay with our staying friends. He asked if he could still get tickets to boxing matches and I said of course. I really did feel sorry for him, but I was no longer his sucker.

I finally had the house to myself. This was the first time I had been alone since I got my apartment in 1990, and I was lonely. A couple of months after Darryl moved out, a friend of mine was breaking up with her boyfriend at the time and I asked her if she wanted to rent a room from me. So my friend Jana moved in. We got along great—we were both easy to live with.

I used to go back and forth a lot to LA. I had friends out there and I started to have an affair with a married man named Louie. Louie had an interesting choice of profession: he was in the air conditioning business by day and a mobster at night. He worked as a captain for a reputed New York crime family. Legitimizing their business was his job. I was treated like a princess, far from the way Darryl treated me. I was mesmerized. We would steal away as much time as we could on weekends and day trips that we made back and forth between LA and Vegas. He was a spoiler, and always came bearing gifts: perfume, jewelry, flowers. Very sweet. I think my favorite gift was the one where a friend of his owned a dry cleaner in Las Vegas and I got my dry cleaning for free. This was a huge savings for someone who only wore dry clean at the time. We even went into business together; we bought a limousine and hired a driver for people to rent hourly for special events, weddings and proms. We had no idea what the hell we were doing and used it for ourselves most of the time but who cared? We were having fun.

Darryl found out that I was seeing someone but he didn't know who, and he was incensed. He followed Louie and me to a bar one night—a little local place called Pepper's Lounge—and Louie was very much a gentleman and told him to run along. That was the beginning of what, for the next year, would be some of the worst memories of my life. Darryl turned into a stalker.

Now I am not talking just a little jealousy; he was psychotic. The meth was altering his personality and he was downright scary. I had always seen these women on TV talk about the horrors of being stalked but I never thought it was as bad as they were making out to be. But it was.

My boss assigned security from the hotel to live in my cottage and watch me around the clock. Darryl was everywhere. He followed me, he called me, and he would wait for me outside the hotel, in the parking garage, outside the house. Before the security detail moved in, he did things like pull a gun or hold a knife to my throat or take a baseball bat to my ribs. One night he got into the house and broke all the glass. I was terrified and I was certain that one day he was going to kill me.

It killed Louie not to be able to take care of the situation like he wanted to. I went as far as to ask for him to take care of Darryl, if you know what I mean, but we were under too much scrutiny and it surely would have landed Louie in jail and I didn't want that. But he did promise me that somehow, he would take care of things, but before he could, he was indicted for murder and I never saw Louie again.

I was finally assigned a detective from the Special Victims Unit at Las Vegas' Metropolitan Police Department and they kept a running tab on all of Darryl's escapades, but it didn't stop him. They were building a case. I said, "Well, while you build your case, I am going to wind up dead." That afternoon my boss called me into his office. Darryl got through to him at the office and filled his head with all the things I had trusted Darryl with about my boss. Well, my boss felt betrayed and said those things I shared with Darryl were told to me in confidence and what if Darryl took those stories and went and talked to his wife? It would surely be the cause of much heartache for him and make his life at home difficult. I was embarrassed and furious. I apologized profusely and threw myself on his mercy. I stormed out of his office and drove to my house and went in the closet and took down my 9mm Glock and put it in my car on the passenger seat. One of the security guys, Luther, came up behind me and thought I seemed just a little off, and then he saw the gun on the seat of the car. He said, "Come on now, Christine, don't ruin your life. Don't do something you're going to regret." On that day, he talked me out of killing Darryl.

# CHAPTER 15
## FOREVER IS RELATIVE
## 1997

By May Darryl had lightened up immensely. The detectives paid him a visit and told him they were pursuing charges for stalking and they were going to be watching him. But he was still a thorn in my side. His excuse to see me was always that he wanted to see the dogs. Finally, I just said, "The hell with it. You know what? Take the dogs. Just leave me alone." And that—finally—was the end of him.

Mimi was now 13 years old, and her health was failing. I did everything I could to prolong her life, but between old age and complications with cancer, she was suffering and I didn't want that. Finally, I got up the courage to bring her to the vet and put her down. The doctor asked me if I wanted to wait outside, but I didn't I didn't want her to be alone, so I stayed, and she died peacefully, with me whispering in her ear that she was a good kitty and I loved her and that my mom and dad would watch her until I could be with her again. I was a wreck when I left that office. I had her cremated and spread her ashes under her favorite tree in the backyard on 15th Street.

My friend Sarah sold cars at a Nissan dealership and sold a car to a guy she thought I would be interested in. She gave him my number and told me he was going to be calling. All she said was that I would be pleased—he's dreamy, looks like a soap opera star. Later that day, I got a call from a guy named Steve. I had my secretary grill him. I had no idea who he was, and she said he said Sarah told him to call. Okay, now I knew who it was—it was my blind date.

We talked quickly. I was on my way to a meeting and we set up to meet for drinks at 7pm that night at Z'tejas, a bar just east of the Strip. I got to Z'tejas, valet parked and ran in. I was wearing work clothes, so I was in a suit, my favorite Donna Karan navy blue pinstripe with a white collar shirt (starched, of course, and compliments of my free dry cleaning, which I still had—it was a lifetime arrangement). He was wearing Levis and a white Calvin Klein v-neck t-shirt with a pair of Nikes. Oh. My. God. He was the most beautiful creature I had laid eyes on to date. Sarah's description didn't do him justice. 6'4", built, fit. Blond hair, blue eyes, outstanding. We had drinks and dinner and we talked about my job and his, and when he said he loved Tom Jones, I said, "Oh, yeah, he's playing this week at the hotel. Would you like to see him?" He was over-the-top excited, and we made plans to see the show the next night. I let him know that I was having surgery—cosmetic surgery—and that this would be the last time I would see him for about a week, but after I was up and around, we could get together. He was intrigued and asked, "What surgery are you having?" I said, "Uh, just a little lypo and a nose job." He was more intrigued. So much so that when I came home after the surgery, he showed up at my house with flowers and sour patch kids, my favorite candy, to take a look for himself. He truly saw me at my worst. I looked like I had two black eyes and I was several different colors, bruised from the lypo.

It was official: Steve and I were dating and exclusive and we were really falling in love. He was just the sweetest guy—so tender and caring—and really took great care of me, emotionally and physically. He was the first man that wasn't a thief, a drug dealer or a mobster. He was a straight-laced working guy who had his shit together. And that was a big change from my past relationships.

Steve asked me to marry him the night Mike Tyson bit Holyfield's ear. He had been acting strange all night. He said he had a bad case of nerves—it was his first live boxing match and he thought I would say no. But I didn't—I said yes—and Steve and I were married in a private ceremony at the Calneva Hotel in Lake Tahoe overlooking the lake on July 12th, just eight short weeks after we started dating.

I hid my marriage from my boss (I knew he would have an allergic reaction), but I couldn't hide it forever and so I told him. My instinct was correct. He went into orbit. He said it was too soon, it was a mistake and I was completely irrational and needed to take my medication. That he had put up with an unstable first husband and he wasn't going to clean up the mess of a mistake of a second husband. I let him have his peace and I told him I was sorry I couldn't have his blessing. What he said next chilled me to the bone: "If you stay with him and don't get divorced immediately, I will fire you. I will ruin you. You will never be able to work anywhere in this town." And I said, "Oh, really, don't threaten me, you can't tell me what to do. In fact, I quit." I didn't think for one second that this wasn't just a heated argument that would blow over, but it didn't and two weeks later, I left the building with a small box of personal belongings. I was officially relieved of my duties and no one would touch me, as I was unemployable. I was ruined.

You're asking yourself why it went down that way. For years, I asked myself why I called his bluff. I knew him best of all. I knew it wasn't an idle threat but it was what it was. The lines were drawn and I crossed them. I made my bed and now I was going to lie in it. When I started at MGM, I never imagined I would leave. I thought I would be there forever. Well, friends, forever is a mighty long time.

About a month after my departure from MGM, my brother called and said my boss called him that evening about my diagnosis, and that he thought I married Steve because I was having an episode. He also told my brother that while I was there, I abused my privileges and that he didn't want to clean up any more of my mistakes. He fired me. My brother didn't give a rat's ass whether I abused my privileges or not. What he was most concerned about was that I had hidden a mental illness for ten years. My answer was I didn't want him to worry and I assured him that I was fine and in therapy and that marrying Steve wasn't my mania—that I really did love him. That seemed to suffice, but I could hear the concern in his voice. And to be honest, I wasn't so sure that I believed what I was saying myself.

# CHAPTER 16
# THERE'S NO TURNING BACK
## 1998–1999

Steve and I didn't think we were going to make it past our first year of marriage. I went into a major depression and there were days I couldn't get out of bed. On top of being depressed, I had a major identity crisis. MGM had become so much a part of who I was as an individual that I didn't know who I was if I didn't go there every day. I couldn't find a job, no one would hire me, and the word was out in the gaming industry that I was damaged goods. There were many times I felt like picking up the phone and groveling for my job back, but I had too much pride and I knew there was no going back.

I never told Steve prior to marrying him that I was manic-depressive; he found that out on his own between the severe depression and my mood swings. He finally just came right out and asked if there was something about my behavior that he needed to know, and I leveled with him and he sat and listened and understood. He wasn't happy that I kept it a secret, but he understood and asked what he could do to help. I told him I needed to continue to go to therapy but that I couldn't because I had no insurance or income. He said he would pay for me to go and would also add me to his insurance. He was as supportive of a husband as you could expect.

Steve was, like me, very much a perfectionist—I with business stuff; he with his body. He proposed I start working out with him, so I did. Every morning, we woke up and hit the gym, and after he was done with work, we'd go back for more. That's how my negative energy got channeled. We did cardio in the morning and weights at night. He also helped me with my diet (we were on a high-protein/low-carb diet and had one cheat day a week).

Steve was working in the lighting industry for a company that supplied street lights to the City of Las Vegas. Lucrative, they were the only game in town back then. Most of his time was spent making deals on the golf course, and he had a schedule flexible enough that he had a lot of time to spend with me. We travelled and took weekend trips to Tahoe and San Diego, just doing fun couples stuff. We always had something to talk about and something to do.

I finally found a job, as an Operations Manager for a manufacturer of "tween" novelty items. It was decent pay and got me out of the house and gave me some sort of purpose. In January of 1999, with my Christmas bonus, I decided to have more cosmetic surgery done. I needed to have the second part of my nose job to make it even smaller, and I was going to have a breast reduction and lift.

The first article was written about me in the Las Vegas Review Journal. I was now infamous; my civil SEC case for Chrysler finally settled. I was charged with tipping (meaning leaking the information) and ordered to pay a $150,000 fine. Darryl was charged with insider trading and ordered to repay his profit plus a $150,000 fine. Neither one of us had that kind of money so we each filed for bankruptcy. Are you keeping count? This is bankruptcy number two. We also both received consent decrees, which ordered us never to commit a securities violation again for as long as we both shall live.

I left the manufacturer in February of 1999 because, truth be told, the people that ran the company were a little weird. I got a job for a few months as an office manager for an architect. That summer, my sister Debbie called to let me know she was asking her husband for a divorce, which floored me, and when I asked why what happened, she said that she had met someone else and she was moving in with her. Did you get that last part? HER. Alright, now how is it that three out of eight siblings are gay? Obviously this has to be in the Anderson genes and not the Favara ones. Yeah, that's it. I hung up the phone and Steve said it looked like I'd seen a ghost. I told him what Debbie had just told me and he said, "WOW, she's a lesbo, that's cool," and he snickered. I said, "You are not getting the point; this is why I'm in therapy. Now I will have to schedule an extra therapy session because of this." And we both laughed.

Also that summer, Darryl was finally tried for stalking me. I testified at the trial, which sealed his fate. He was sentenced to one year in a state facility and mandatory drug rehabilitation. I never saw or heard from Darryl again.

I kept looking for a better-paying job and made a contact that offered me a position as a Vice President for the Nevada Development Authority. My position was to help the state diversify the economy from gaming, and create non-gaming jobs by attracting new companies to Southern Nevada. My assigned area of expertise was to be in the dot-coms and startups. This was a great gig: I was making close to $90,000 with my bonuses and I had full benefits.

I got right into the groove at my job and I just loved it—it was really right up my alley. I had a great networking base and was making a name for myself on my own this time. I wasn't in someone's shadow. I was at the top of my game and when I was "on," there was no one better.

I turned 30 that September and I was feeling nostalgic. I had been gone from MGM for two years. I read that day in the newspaper that my former boss had left the hotel and moved to Los Angeles to run the movie studio, so I extended the olive branch and I called him to congratulate him. I don't know what I expected, but he immediately took my call, so I told him that I was happy for him and that I wished him well. I said, "The next time you're in Vegas, maybe we can have a drink?" And he said, "I'm in Vegas right now. Meet me at the hotel for dinner at 7pm in the Mansion and we'll catch up. I'd love to see you."

I called Steve and explained. He encouraged the meeting—that it would be good closure. And it was. My former boss and I both commented that the other looked good and happy. He said I should screen-test for a Bond girl. We talked about how our lives were now and how crazy our lives were then. I took the opportunity to tell him how much I appreciated him and that I called mostly because I never wanted something to happen to him without his knowing that I loved him for all he had done for me and that I was a better person because of him. That the education he gave me was priceless. We finished our dinners and said our goodbyes and as I drove off in my car, I felt that I had righted a wrong and was at peace.

# CHAPTER 17
## NEW ERA, NEW ME
## 2000–2001

**W**e celebrated the Millennium with our friends at a private party at the Golden Nugget in downtown Las Vegas. I was a slim 135 pounds, wearing a size four. I let my hair grow long and dyed it blonde, very blonde. I had a new nose and new boobs. I looked good and I knew it.

Men were hitting on me all the time and frankly, I enjoyed all the attention. I started to, as they say, act like my "shit didn't stink" as all of the attention was getting to my head. I was gorgeous and confident and I felt sexy. Steve had created a monster.

I was in the middle of starting a website of my own called TheSiliconOasis.com, which is now a networking portal for technology companies for Nevada, and I worked long hours and did a lot of networking. I was meeting a lot of men. My hormones kicked into overdrive and what I did next was inexcusable—for the next year. I slept with everything that walked. I had so many affairs and one-night stands that I could not even begin to remember names or how many to give you the details in this book. I went as far as to have an experience with another woman, to see if there was something to this whole lesbian thing. No, definitely not in the Anderson genes.

You're waiting to find out if Steve was a bad guy and if I had a good reason. To my shame, he wasn't. He was the best husband anyone could ever ask for and I am sure his wife today would agree. I was just selfish and only cared about how I felt and what I needed. I never once thought about him. Doctors say it was my mania, that I did it because it made me feel invincible and powerful. I say I did it because I could.

Steve asked me for a divorce in January of 2001, after one of my trysts made it into the society page of the Las Vegas Review Journal. He was crushed. I couldn't argue with him—I was terrible and what I had done was unforgiveable. We did the divorce ourselves. I gave him the house on 15th Street, a new Mercedes we had bought, and, except for a few pieces of art and my clothes and the $50,000 in cash we had in the bank, I left everything else behind.

My brother was so concerned by what I was telling him that he flew out on his own and demanded a meeting with my therapist. Sue told him it wasn't that he did a poor job raising me; this was just how I was. I was genetically predisposed to the disorder and there was nothing anyone could do to make things different.

I rented a three-bedroom house on Coppola Street in the Southern Highlands section of Las Vegas just southwest of the Strip. My brother stayed long enough to help me move. My old friend Jana moved back in with me to keep me company and out of trouble. I got myself a dog, a solid black German Shepherd I named Mykos. I bought him at a pet shop for $700, and I told myself it was a rescue because the conditions of the pet shop were so awful.

I made a contact at the development authority who recruited me to work for him at a startup technology company called Sattrac. It sounded promising and I was a risk taker so I went for it. I was making more money and I bought my first BMW, a nice, silver 330i. I was quite content living in my little house, driving my Beemer.

We were getting busy at Sattrac and needed an extra set of hands. My boss hired an analyst he met at a conference to help with the business plan and web development and to crunch some numbers. Ryan was a nice kid. I could say kid now that I was in my 30s, and he was in his early 20s.

It was summer and Ryan wasn't working there more than a couple of weeks when he announced that he had a friend in LA named Chris, a musician coming to Vegas who wanted to meet me because he saw my picture and liked my blonde hair and big boobs. We set it up. I would make a nice Italian-style dinner at my house and he would come over for a home-cooked meal. We met on a Sunday, and it was kismet. We were both smitten. We had a nice dinner at my house (I made lasagna) and then went to the House of Blues Foundation Room, a private members-only club at the top of Mandalay Bay, for dessert. Chris wanted to go gambling downtown so we headed to the Golden Nugget and played a few hands of blackjack. It was 1am and his plane left at 11am, so we decided to call it a night and headed back to my house where we had the most outstanding sex I have had to date. I mean, the guy knew his way around. We slept for a couple of hours, and then we got up and I dropped him off at the airport and we made plans for me to go to LA and stay at his place the next weekend. Chris and I started going back and forth between the cities and were dating and having a blast.

Mykos and I used to go to the doggie park a lot. I had a small yard and it was good to get him socialized with other animals. One day, I realized, as I was sitting there by myself, that there was a Doberman puppy at the park with no owner. I went around asking if it was anyone's and it wasn't. I waited an hour to see if anyone showed up to claim him and no one ever did. I took him home. I went back that evening and put flyers up that I had found a male black and tan Dobie puppy and if it was anyone's, to contact me. No one ever did so I kept him and named him Zeus and took at as a sign from God that my father was sending me Zeus to watch over me. Not long after I got Zeus, I donated Mykos to the Las Vegas Metropolitan Police Department K9 unit. He was showing signs of aggression and a friend that worked there thought he would be perfect. Mykos retired with his partner in 2010.

It was the fall of 2000 and my boss and I were meeting with investors trying to raise startup capital for Sattrac when in walked the devil himself—Barclay. I have an affinity for older men—I get it from my mother. And here he was: a handsome, distinguished man in his late 50s with a full head of silver hair—a man that made my heart skip a beat. Did I mention he had been married for 25 years? I didn't care. I went in for the kill. I just wanted to jump his bones.

Barclay and I were flirting during the meeting and after it was over, he pulled me aside and asked me if I wanted to join him at the Mandalay Bay for a drink. I said sure and we made plans to meet at the main bar at 8 that evening.

We sat and talked for a few hours and he told me about a company that he had invested in, an OTCBB company (small cap stock that is publicly traded on the Over the Counter Bulletin Board Exchange), and it was turning out to be a bad investment. He was trying to figure out what he should do with it and wanted my opinion, as it seemed like I knew my stuff in the meeting earlier that day and he wanted a new perspective. I told him I thought they need to identify a merger or acquisition candidate, and that organically growing the business obviously wasn't working, but without seeing the business plan and the numbers, I was just guessing. And so the deal with the devil was made. And I sold my soul.

It was decided that night that I would come on to Premiere as a consultant and help them identify a merger or acquisition candidate and see the deal through. In return, I would be paid $5,000 per month in consulting fees, and oh, I was to be his mistress and at his beck and call and be kept in the lifestyle to which MGM had me accustomed. We went up to a VIP suite and consummated the deal, the proverbial handshake.

I gave notice at Sattrac and took Ryan with me. I needed someone I could trust to help me with this project and it was a great opportunity. It also meant that I would be in LA more often and could see Chris. I told Barclay if he could be married, I could have Chris. He agreed. Chris was on tour most of the year and we spent holidays separately.

It was the end of January 2001. Barclay planned a trip to meet with the stock promoters in New York and made plans to stay for a week at the Plaza in the presidential suite. Barclay may have been the devil, but he had class and good taste. He gave me great gifts. Awesome jewelry. And he always took me shopping at my favorite boutique, Escada. It was nothing for him to drop $10,000 on clothes for me. During our meetings, everyone had the same comment: the president of the company didn't know what he was doing and it made investors skeptical and that's why they were having problems pitching the story. Barclay listened and made mental notes and after our time was up in New York, and we had visited with my family, we headed back to Vegas were he began the coup. He flew to LA a week after we returned to New York to let the current president know he was relieved of his duties and that the board wanted his resignation. Two weeks later. I was made President and CEO at the ripe old age of 32. Who says you can't sleep your way to the top?

I ran Premiere from my home office in Vegas and flew into the Beverly Hills office weekly, and by summer, I identified an acquisition target. I was setting us up to take over Axium, which was a payroll company that did movie-specific payrolls in the entertainment industry. This was a huge win for us. We began our meetings and research and diligence into Axium's operations and books and were a couple months into our process when the unimaginable happened—9/11.

I was physically sick. I had so many friends and business associates. Calls weren't going through, and phone lines were dead. The scenes on the news were terrifying. That is when the world as we know it changed forever.

The stock plummeted, my deal went south, and we had nothing in the aftermath of 9/11, either as a country or as a company. There was only one thing I could do: move to LA. The company needed me full-time. I needed it to recover for all of our sakes; our paychecks were on the line. I called my brother, told him I was moving to LA, and asked if he could help with the move. He got on a plane, and I was in LA for the first of October. Hollywood, here I come.

Me and Mom
'74

Me, Dad and
King
'76

Communion
'76

Mom and Dad dancing at
Bobby's wedding
'73

*Last time we were all together
for Bobby's wedding
73*

*Grammar School
Graduation
'84*

*High School
Graduation
'87*

*My first year at MGM*
*'92*

*Married to Darryl*
*'93*

*Married to Steve*
*'99*

Hollywood Hills Home
2002

Prison
2010

Me and Sam,
Home in Virginia
2013

# Part IV
# LA-la Land

*"Beware of temptation that success brings. There is grave danger in getting what we want."*
—Philip Yancey

# CHAPTER 18
# I'M READY FOR MY CLOSE-UP, MR. DEMILLE
# 2001

C hris found me an awesome place to rent: the cottage that belonged to Charlie Chaplin in a place called Chaplin Court on Formosa Avenue in Hollywood. Chaplin Court was built in the 20s during the Silent Movie Era when Chaplin had his own studio on La Brea Avenue, and this particular compound was comprised of four cottages that housed the actors in the films—people like Barrymore and Fairbanks and Hemmingway, Hollywood legends. I had a two-bedroom, two-bath, two-story cottage with a small backyard for Zeus, and the courtyard was gated so I used to let Zeus out in the common area to play. I was about a 20-minute drive through city streets to my office on Wilshire Boulevard in Beverly Hills; my commute was a no-brainer. I still had my BMW, but I bought a 2001 Corvette just because, and the company had its own limo and driver.

The move went pretty smoothly. I had spent so much time in LA over the years that it just seemed like a natural progression. Deep down, I was really done with Vegas and needed to move on.

I was referred to a therapist in LA by Sue Daniel—a Dr. Linda Barnes in Beverly Hills. I went and met with her and discussed my medical history. She asked me a session's worth of questions and at the end of the session, I asked if she found anything different in her diagnosis than my previous two doctors had. She said no, that she would have to concur with the previous findings and agree that I was indeed Bipolar I. She asked what medication I was taking and I said I had never really taken my medication more than a couple of weeks at a time and I was famous for starting and stopping all the time. She then referred me to a psychiatrist for my medication named Dr. Rebecca Crandall (in the Brentwood section of LA) and I made an appointment to see her the next day.

My visit with Dr. Crandall went well and I was comfortable with her immediately. She said she could prescribe medication as well as provide therapy, so there was no need to see Linda Barnes anymore unless I wanted to. I decided that I would see Dr. Crandall for both meds and therapy, and simplify my life by not having to go to two doctors. She said she understood from Dr. Barnes that I was not compliant with my medication and I, of course, agreed. She said she wanted me to give it the good old college try, and asked me what I did to sleep. I told her I didn't do anything; I just stayed up and dealt with the insomnia. She said she would prescribe both the Lithium at 1200mg and Prozac at 60mg like Dr. Laborati, but she was going to change my Ativan to Xanax at .5mg and the Xanax should help with the anxiety and sleep.

I tried the medication. I took them faithfully for the next six months and I blew up like a balloon. I went from an 8 to a 14. I couldn't stand the sight of myself again. Chris said it wasn't attractive and Barclay said it wasn't appealing. I stopped my medicine. All but the Xanax . . . now those I liked.

# Chapter 19
# The Best Things in Life Aren't Always Free
# 2002

Our acquisition of Axium was dead. It was time to move on, but the country wasn't ready, the markets were in the toilet, and investors were spooked by 9/11. I had started researching other options, when a friend of Barclay's (who also was the President of a publicly traded company) told me that he was getting funding from a company in Chicago that used the 144 shares (which is restricted stock used for consultants and employees who earned stock and have been with the company two years or more). Basically, what I had to do was pay the company lending us the money in stock for their services. Sounded okay to me. I would give them stock, which didn't cost me anything, and they would give me money. What could be wrong with this arrangement?

I flew to Chicago to meet with Frank Custable of Suburban Capital. We hit it off right away, and I liked him both personally and professionally. We knew that what we were planning on doing was illegal, but we never said the words out loud. Here is what was illegal: he never really supplied legitimate consulting services, and I never really had any employees who were there over two years. I was simply giving him enough stock to make me whole and make some for himself.

Back then, I said the reason I made this deal was because I would do anything to save the company, but the truth was I didn't want to be known as a failure.

I would go out to Chicago every six weeks, have dinner, talk a little business, make the expense reports look good, and fly back home. I never stayed more than a couple of days. By this time, Custable explained that in order for him to unload the stock developed into the open market, I would have to issue press releases every so often to the Street that would detail plans for the company to make acquisitions or mergers. I would also have to say that we had new business and our projected earnings and revenue were "X" million instead of the few thousands that they actually were. I sent out 26 such bogus releases between 2002 and 2003.

In the meantime, we were approaching summer in LA, the money was rolling in, and I was blowing it as fast as it came in. I had every piece in the Escada line that year and I was making my mark at Tiffany's and Chanel. I enjoyed the finer things and loved being able to walk into a store, point at an item and say, "I will take that" without so much as blinking at the price. In fact, I often didn't ask how much—I just presented a card when it was rung up.

It was about this time I started sending $5,000 month to my brother to help him make his life easier. I had it so I felt it was the least I could do.

My sister Barbara also needed some help. She was between jobs and her credit cards were maxed. I paid off her Discover Card—$15,000. This was the first of three times that I paid that damn card. She was also in need of some experimental medical drug at the time, Interferon, and that was $1,000 month. I paid for that as well, on top of car insurance and car payments when she needed those. I did what I could when I could for anyone who asked; that just the way I was. I felt I was fortunate enough to have, so why not share?

Custable sent a wire once a week, but it was becoming more and more difficult to pinpoint which day. I got into a bad habit of kiting checks. I knew if a check bounced, it would be presented three more times before it would be returned and considered "bad", so I constantly pushed the envelope.

I was at my usual spot at the Escada store in the Beverly Wilshire picking out a few new pieces and, unbeknownst to me, the check I had written the week before bounced for $25,000 (give or take a few pennies). Two Beverly Hills cops arrested me right there on the spot, took my Fendi checkbook, put me in cuffs and gently placed me in the back of their patrol car. I had no idea what I was arrested for—it could have been anything. I just stayed quiet, and when it came time to make a call, I called Ryan and my secretary Yvonne, and they came and bailed me out. I had enough cash in my purse to pay the bail bondswoman they hired, and I was sent home that evening after just a few hours.

I was arrested for writing a bad check—a felony—but if my kiting estimates were right, this check was definitely paid the following week when the wire came in. The first thing I did was call Barclay; surely he would know what to do and have an attorney I could call. When I did, I found out that he had gone down to the Federal Building in Las Vegas that morning and self-surrendered to begin a five-year prison sentence. He had been found guilty of a pump-and-dump scheme about a month prior for a scam he ran during the time of the Clintons' Whitewater scandal. I wasn't surprised; I knew he was preoccupied since I was seeing less and less of him. I made a call to the only attorney I knew, Oscar Goodman, and he referred me to an attorney in Los Angeles, Anthony Brooklier. Tony was most famous for representing Heidi Fleiss, so I figured if it's good enough for the "Hollywood Madame," it's good enough for me.

I went the next day to his office in Century City and he asked if I could, in fact, prove the check was paid, and I told him I could. He said, "Okay, well, since you're a friend of Oscar's, give me $5,000 and we'll get this taken care of for you." I handed him the money and he was true to his word, back and forth a few times to Beverly Hills Court. The charges were dismissed, and he has forever since called me the "Escada Bandit" and warned me that, in prison, Escada isn't available.

By the end of 2002, Custable's money source all but dried up. He was under investigation by the feds and it just didn't seem like a good idea to continue the relationship, so I started looking for new blood—someone who could do the same thing.

October of this year, I moved to a house that I found on the way to taking Zeus to his usual doggie park, up in the Hollywood Hills on Tahoe Drive. It was a four-bedroom, four-bath two-story with an in-ground pool overlooking Lake Hollywood, with a breathtaking view of the city and the Hollywood sign. I spent at least $250,000 decorating and furnishing. Obviously I had the best and spared no expense. I had several vehicles at this point, and rarely did you catch me in the same one twice in a week. I also bought myself two pedigree Chihuahuas, Louie and Gina, who were adorable. Zeus loved having the company.

I found a guy in Florida to takeover for Custable, and he was good to send anything between $25,000–50,000 a week. Things kept moving along. But the business was suffering, as my lavish lifestyle was draining it. It used to be the business was first, and then I got what was left over. Now it was the other way around. We had closed the office in Beverly Hills and we were working out of an office in my house. I converted the garage to accommodate myself and four employees.

The SEC requested the honor of my presence again. I was represented by a decent SEC attorney, Irv Einhorn. Honestly, all I needed him to do was sit there with me while I said over and over that on the advice of counsel, I was asserting my Fifth Amendment privilege on the grounds that my answers might incriminate me. Catherine Whiting, the SEC agent, wasn't amused. I got the feeling she just didn't like me. This went on for about four hours then they called it quits.

That Christmas, I had a Black Tie company party at my house. White glove catering, valet, the house professionally decorated. I flew my brother out, and that was the first time he saw my mini mansion and fleet of cars, and he couldn't have been prouder. If he only had known it was all a façade.

# Chapter 20
# All Good Things Must Come to an End
# 2003

By February I couldn't hold it together. The kid I was using in Florida dried up and there was no money coming in. I did the only thing I knew how to do: sell my assets. I called Custable and told him I wanted to sell the business and I was looking to get $250,000 for it. He said he would see what he could do. A couple of weeks later, I sold the publicly traded entity (what we call in the business a "shell") to a guy out of Indiana who wanted to take his guitar manufacturing company public. But he didn't know the ropes of running a publicly traded company and asked if I could stay on in a consulting capacity for six months. I agreed to stay on for my original consulting fee of $5,000 per month, plus they would pay me $10,000 up front for the shell, then the balance of $240,000 over the next six months (in installments of 40,000 per month). My insurance that I would be paid was the amount they owed equal in unrestricted stock because I had earned it working for the company for the past two-and-a-half years, so my Regulation 144 stock was, in fact, free and clear.

That's when my subpoenas were served by the Postal Inspector. The grand jury was convening to see if there was enough evidence to indict me on securities fraud charges. They wanted my files as part of the discovery process and if I didn't send them, they would come and get them. It took us about a week to get them everything they were asking for. We sent it all over to Tony, who was going to put the finishing touches on it "legalese wise" and send it off the Department of Justice. I remember thinking at that point, 'They'll never be able to figure it out.'

The mortgage on my house alone was $4,000.00. I had put a significant amount down in cash, but left a small mortgage for the tax write-off. The cars were paid for; I started to sell them off one by one, but kept the Mercedes and the Explorer. It cost double what I was making in consulting fees to just run that house every month between the mortgage, utilities, taxes and my personal assistant and housekeeper. It was a drain but I wasn't going down without a fight so I held on. In waiting for the monies to come from the payment of the sale of Premiere, I was racking up credit card debt, not in my name but in Chris'. By the end of the summer, we had $96,000 in credit card bills and no payments in sight.

I knew I needed to generate other income since I would burn through this money pretty quickly. I hired a business broker to find me a good cash business that we could put me in the positive. Finally, the payments started coming in from the sale of Premiere. It came in one lump sum but heck, I didn't care. As long as I got my money, I didn't care how I got it. I remember Chris couldn't believe the bills were paid. He said he would never doubt me again. We'll see about that.

That October, I severed my consulting agreement and purchased a 30-year-old flower shop out in the Valley that was being sold because it was a family business and they were retiring. I drove out with my assistant and we fell in love with it. It was a charming shop with a good customer base in the Sylmar section of Los Angeles. I made them an offer of $75,000, which was about $10,000 less than their asking price. I said I had cash and I could close quickly, and they accepted. In an instant, I went from socialite to shopkeeper. Depressing.

# CHAPTER 21
# EVERYTHING'S COMING UP ROSES
# 2004

I was putting in crazy hours trying to wrap my arms around the day-to-day operations of the business. I had my assistant, a designer and a driver. We were FTD and Teleflora, and it was a good little business.

I was losing the house in the Hills. I just couldn't afford it. Out of the money I received for the sale, I paid $96,000 in credit card and $75,000 for the cost of the business, which left me $75,000 in the bank. It was going fast; my lifestyle hadn't changed. I was still going out to expensive dinners, buying presents for others, paying people's bills, helping them out of jams, shopping at Escada. I was also buying things for the business, like business cards and stationery and inventory, all in cash. By the end of spring, I had $10,000 left in the bank and I lost the house in the hills. Foreclosure.

I moved to a rental house in Sylmar, a nice three-bedroom, two-bath ranch, but a serious downgrade from where I had been living. I felt like I had just taken a step back in time and I was on Clinton Avenue again. I mean, what's next—food stamps? I had to do something, and quick, so I got on Craigslist. I always heard if you married an immigrant and got them their papers, they would pay good money. I was desperate. I answered an ad and that when I met Ronald.

Ronald was a dental student from Lebanon, studying with a doctor in Beverly Hills with the hopes of getting his license and establishing a practice once he was here legally. Remember, this is business, people. We shook hands, and for $25,000, he would become husband number three.

Chris thought I had completely lost my mind. I had to tell him, right? Obviously he would come home from the road, and there would be a man living with me. He said this time, I had gone too far, and I said, marry me then and I won't go through with it. And he said absolutely not—he was never marrying, for one, and if he was going to get married, it wasn't going to be to someone as crazy as me. A very valid reason.

Ronald and I got married in the Beverly Hills Courthouse that summer and he moved in and it lasted one month to the day. Chris gave me an ultimatum: Ronald goes or I go. I backed out of the deal and returned the money. All in the name of love. Love for Chris, that is. Ronald moved out and Chris was around more, like he'd promised, but he wasn't moving in. We just continued to do what we had always done—spend a night or two here or there and see each other when he was home from the road or not in the studio. And it worked for us.

This was the year I got Kiwi, my yellow-naped Amazon parrot that I still have with me today. My gynecologist in Beverly Hills called me and knew I rescued animals and asked if I could take Kiwi—he had found him in an abandoned apartment and couldn't keep him. So I had my driver go to Beverly Hills and pick him up. Just what I needed . . . a bird that would repeat everything I say.

# Chapter 22
# You Can Run but You Can't Hide
# 2005

**B**usiness was booming. I added 1-800-Flowers and we were doing fantastic. I added another driver and another designer and we had two delivery vehicles: my old Explorer and a brand-new Ford van for event pieces. I did have a knack for running a business and making it profitable, but make no mistake—I made sure I got mine. Of course my employees always came first and I was generous to a fault. No one can ever dispute that. I had to do the unthinkable: Zeus had been sick. He had a rare form of skin cancer and he was becoming aggressive. He had bitten three people, but it was to the point where it wasn't safe to have him, for fear that someone would get seriously injured, so I made the decision to put him down. I was beside myself for weeks. I missed him terribly. I had him cremated and I took him up to the doggie park by the house in the hills and spread his ashes under his favorite tree.

The business grew at such a fast pace that, financially, it was difficult to keep up cash flow-wise. Receivables always took so long to collect and we were always 30 days in arrears. I opened lines of credit and bought the van all under Chris' name. He had good credit because of me so I figured what he didn't know wouldn't hurt him. I paid the bills anyway. He would only find out if I didn't, and that would never happen . . . would it?

Chris went to a Wells Fargo branch in Phoenix. He was there for work and needed to make a withdrawal. The teller asked if he wanted to make a payment on his credit line because it was overdue. Oh, damn. He called and was furious and I couldn't get a word in edgewise and he hung up. In bed a few nights later, after he was back in LA, he neglected to tell me he had gone to the police and filed a report for identity theft.

About a month later, at the end of April, I was pulled over because my tail light was out. When they ran my license, I had an outstanding warrant. They didn't say for what—just that they had to take me in.

Off to San Fernando Jail I went. I made the usual calls to the bail bondswoman I'd used before, and to Tony, my attorney. In a few hours, I was released on bond. The charge? Identity theft. I was going to kill Chris. Not literally, but I was fuming.

I called Chris—it must have been two or three in the morning—and he was just getting in, and I said "Guess where I was tonight?" He said, "I don't know, where?" "In San Fernando Jail. I was arrested for identity theft." Silence. I said, "Hello?" He said, "I didn't think they would really do anything about that." I said, "Well, surprise. You better come with me tomorrow and get my car out of impound and then to Tony's. You'd better fix this."

The next day and $350.00 later, I had my Mercedes back and Chris promised Tony that he would call the DA and convince him to drop the charges. A month later, the charges were dropped. "The witness failed to cooperate," the DA said. I bet he did.

Middle of May and things seem as normal as normal can be; then I get the call that forever changed my life. It was Tony. He said, "Why didn't you tell me you were getting indicted?" I said, "I don't think that I am." He said, "This indictment that just came through my fax says different. You and about eight other people." I said, "Who else is on it?" And he read the names. That was enough. I knew what it was. I said, "What do I do?" He said, "Well, come to my office tomorrow and I'll show it to you and we'll talk about it, but you have to be in Chicago next Tuesday for an arraignment and bond hearing."

I went to Tony's the next day and read it for myself. What I could I do? I was caught, but I wasn't going to give up. I said I wanted to fight it. He suggested I find an attorney in Chicago, that I needed someone who knew the players and was right there in case anything had to be done. I did some research online and found an attorney in Chicago, who I thought, from his profile and our phone conversation, would be great. I retained him verbally and we made plans to meet Tuesday morning before court at his office so I could give him his retainer and go over a few things.

That Monday I flew to Chicago. In my hotel room, the night before my arraignment, I got on my knees and begged God to be merciful and let them grant me bond, and that if he did this for me, I would straighten up and fly right.

The next morning, I showed up at my new attorney John Muldoon's office and we talked and walked over to the Disken Federal Building, where we appeared in front of the District Judge, who granted us all bond, released on our own recognizance on just our signature. However, we would have to remain on Pretrial Supervision until our trial. After we were dismissed, we were processed in the Marshall's office and sent to meet with pretrial. Pretrial notified me that this was a formality, that my supervision would actually take place in California, and that tomorrow, I needed to report to the pretrial office in the Federal Building in Los Angeles at 9am.

I flew home that evening, grateful and thanking God. I was exhausted when I got in, took a Xanax and passed out. When I got up in the morning, I headed down to the pretrial office in the Roybal Federal Building, and the officer went over the conditions of my release, which seemed like a tall order but it beat the alternative.

That July I signed my Injunction for the SEC. I agreed to pay a substantial amount of money in fines and restitution and I agreed to a lifetime bar from the penny stock industry. That meant I could never be an officer and director of a publicly traded company ever again and I could not so much as look at a penny stock on the over-the-counter bulletin board for as long as I lived and breathed. I could never defraud an innocent shareholder again.

Well, folks, I was suicidal. I called Dr. Crandall and I told her I couldn't take it anymore, that I wanted to kill myself, and could I come in to see her? She told me to get in my car, make no stops, and drive straight to her office. I made what is normally a 40-minute drive in 20.

We sat and we talked, or better yet, I unloaded. She had heard all this before and, of course, asked the rhetorical question: "You're not on your medication, are you"? I said, "No, I'm only taking the Xanax to sleep." She prescribed 2mg of Xanax, an increase from the 1mg I was currently taking. She talked me out of killing myself that night. I don't know that I would have really gone through with it, but I was at my limit . . . I was a ticking time bomb.

# Chapter 23
## Never Make A Promise to God You Can't Keep
## 2006

I was growing bored with everything—the flower shop, Chris. I needed to do something interesting so I had this brilliant idea: I would start an escort service. I called it Just for Tonight. I had a couple of people interested in it and a few people made investments, but it never went anywhere or did anything. One of my many flights of fancy.

I met a friend that year. He was an LAPD detective and we slept together one time. Honestly, I wasn't interested in him that way. You know when you should just be friends with someone because they don't do anything else for you? That how I felt about Eric; he, on the other hand, adored me.

I also began sleeping with Josh, an Israeli guy from Beverly Hills. We were pretty hot and heavy. We used to go back and forth to Vegas and I would ask for a line of credit while I was gambling. I would sit and game an average of seven hours at a time at $750 per hand in Blackjack. That year, I racked up $75,000 in casino markers, meaning I borrowed money from the casino.

Money was tight. I was borrowing from everyone I could and paying them back as fast I could. My sister Barbara gave me a diamond ring and Rolex to sell so I could make payroll a couple of times. Things were getting bad. I just had no self-control. I remember Chris said he needed a new car, and I went out and bought him one. I had no business doing it, but I couldn't say no.

The everyday pressures of life that I could normally slough off were wearing me down. I was always paranoid that my phones were tapped or my house was bugged and that people were following me. I contacted psychics on a regular basis and pried them for information as to what would be my fate. No one knew what lay ahead, and this fascination and expectation of being able to predict my future were all symptoms of my mania. I went so far this year as to hire 24-hour security, so I was never alone and had someone with me 24/7. Then I got it in my head that it was because they knew where I was and if I moved, no one would find me. I moved back to Hollywood to the Chaplin Cottage. I remember one night, in one of my most manic states, I called Loretta, whom I hadn't spoken to in what had to be ten years. I told her maybe I would come for a visit, but I never did. I was too afraid to leave my house, let alone the state.

When I told Dr. Crandall that I had 24-hour security, she reined me in and had me come in twice a week. Dr. Crandall recommended I get involved in some kind of activity, something to take me away from it all. So I went that weekend and I bought myself a beautiful Appaloosa named CoCo. Dr. Crandall was right: I started to feel good. The fresh air and getting away from the problems of the shop—it was all good. I enjoyed being with my horse and riding so much (it truly is one of my greatest pleasures even today) that I bought another to keep him company, a black Percheron just a year old, and he was so darn cute I named him Fancy Pants because his tail and mane were curly. Then I began to do research on horse rescue and put some feelers out and before I knew it, I had five horses. When I told Dr. Crandall, she said, "You don't think you're manic? You've purchased five horses inside of a month. How are you going to pay for all this?" I said, "I'm going to sell the shop and with the money I get from the sale, I'm going to start a non-profit and do horse rescue." I told her that this would help me find meaning in my life again. She rolled her eyes and threw her head back and groaned. What could she do—commit me?

I sold the shop—a florist in the next city bought my book of business—and found someone to sublet my lease on the commercial space. I took the proceeds and rented enough space at Circle K Riding Stables to pay their mortgage. The community at the stable was pretty close-knit, but they welcomed me and applauded my efforts for rescuing horses. Some even volunteered their time and helped me with turn-outs and feeding.

I will have you know the $100,000 I sold my business for was all but gone, and the checks I was writing to repay loans or bills were bouncing. I wrote my sister Barbara a check for the $7,000 I got from the sale of her jewelry to pay her back, like I said I would, and that bounced, and if I tell you what she did, you won't believe me. She called my pretrial officer and told her I'd given her a bad check and that I had money hidden in an overseas account, which is how I continued to live my lavish lifestyle, and that I should be arrested. This is the same sister whose credit card I paid three times and kept alive when she needed medicine. I mean, come on. I would have never done something like that no matter how pissed I was, but hey, that's me. I got called in to Chicago and brought up on a violation hearing. Thank God the judge saw that it was more a sibling disagreement than a case of trying to pass a bad check or defraud the government.

The money was almost gone. I was down to my last few dollars, which were spent on riding equipment and tack and feed and vets and farriers. Some of it was necessary, but most of it was just excess. It made perfect sense at the time—at least, that's what you tell yourself when you're manic. But really, did I need a different saddle for each horse? Did I have to color-coordinate all their halters and leads? I think not. I did the only thing I could—I filed for bankruptcy. Yes, folks, that's right, for a third time. So much for straightening up and flying right.

# Part V
# The Inevitable

*"Everything that has happened had to happen. Everything that must happen cannot be stopped."*
—Wayne Dyer

# CHAPTER 24
# ANIMALS ARE SUPPOSED TO
# BE THERAPEUTIC
# 2007

**B**y March of 2007 I was barely treading water; the cost of maintaining the horses was killing me. My labor of love, which was supposed to return the meaning to my life, was becoming a chore. I moved from the Chaplin Cottage to a more "modest" apartment in the Korea Town section of Los Angeles on Berendo Street. My sister Debbie helped me rent it because my latest bankruptcy annihilated my credit. I put an ad on Craigslist for a roommate and a really sweet girl from Canada moved in and we split everything 50/50.

I had so many horses that renting at a public stable became cost-prohibitive, so I rented a private barn on Allen Street in Glendale, just across from the Los Angeles Equestrian Center. By this point I had CoCo, Fancy Pants, plus ten more. In addition to my horses, I added six chickens for good measure. I had also purchased a pedigree Doberman for $2,500 and named him Max.

I had long since placed an ad on Craigslist for some volunteers. I needed some help, you know, to groom and muck and exercise. I wound up with a couple of solid people, some of whom I still keep in touch with today.

I was desperate and had no means of income. Donations were far and few between. I brainstormed and came up with an idea: how about I take all of the credit card receipts from the flower shop and start charging people's credit cards? The deposit will go in overnight and by the time they ask for a refund, because of an error in billing, I would have spent the money and the only person I would owe money to would be the credit card processor. One problem: I don't have a credit card processing account anymore, as that got closed with the store. I asked one of the guys who volunteered at the rescue, whom I'd become friendly with, to go on the corporation with me and let me use his credit to get the account and he agreed. Of course, he didn't know what my plans were; he just thought I would be processing donations. A week later, I was in business.

I could breathe again. I wasn't prepared for the inquiries, and people were calling to dispute charges and get refunds. It was pretty ugly. I would just politely say it was an error and we would credit them immediately. Some people would just take me at face value and never call again, while others were relentless.

It was July and I was on the prowl for a new lover. Chris was still very much in the picture but as usual, I was bored and needed entertainment. I hit Craigslist up to see what I could find. I went to Long Beach to meet a guy on the Queen Mary and we hit it off. He was ten years my junior, which was different, but I liked it. He asked what I did for a living. I told him I was a portfolio manager and I only did high net worth individuals on a one-on-one basis. I asked what he did and he said he grew pot for medicinal purposes and was completely legitimate. I had never met a legitimate drug dealer before so this was intriguing. So intriguing that I obtained a medical marijuana card and asked him to grow some pot for me, and I became a regular smoker, smoking at least two joints per day.

We had been dating for a few weeks when he mentioned that his parents were wealthy and that they were interested in talking to me about a company for which I was doing some consulting and investor relations. I said sure, I will tell them all about it. I spoke to his parents and, although they weren't interested in the company I was consulting for, they were interested in me, and asked if I could recommend some stock for them to buy. I said I could and if they wanted to open accounts, we could do so through my bank and I would send them monthly statements and give them daily or weekly updates by phone. They said, "Sure, we have several accounts with our broker—give us some time to talk to him about it and move things around and we'll be in touch."

By the end of September, they transferred $160,000 to me, which I, in turn, invested it in a portfolio of stocks that I picked. The investments were, in all truth, doing well. But in my mind, I saw this as an opportunity—hey, if I borrow the money and put it back before anyone notices in a few months, I can sell the stock I still have in my own portfolio. Yeah, that collateral stock from the sale of Premiere that I never exercised or returned. Yes, this could work. I liquidated all of the assets and by the end of September, I had $155,000 in my bank account. I was driving a Land Rover and a new Range Rover was on its way.

I had enough money at this point to make a move, so I started looking for a bigger property to rent in the Valley and found a five-acre ranch in the Sunland section of the San Fernando Valley, which was a rent-to-own situation for $4,500 per month. A portion of the rent went toward the $4,000,000 purchase price. My credit was shot, so I used Chris' to do the deal. He didn't know it at the time. The ranch needed some work to be able to house all of those horses and I couldn't do it alone. I hired a trainer that I was using to work for me full-time and act as ranch manager, and I also hired a ranch hand.

I ended my relationship with my lover from Long Beach. Honestly, he had anger issues and just wasn't my cup of tea. I had some remorse; after all,

I did use him for his parents' money. And contrary to popular belief, I had a conscience and felt bad. But this was business and it was just a loan.

By the middle of October, I moved into my ranch on River Wood Lane. It was a beautiful, picturesque piece of property nestled in the Los Angeles Crest Mountains, a gated community of all 5–10-acred ranch homes. Everyone lived onsite except the housekeeper. We began construction in November. We ordered new fencing and converted some of the pasture into stall space for boarding, but my most favorite addition was going to be a 70' round pen, completely enclosed and made out of wood for training. To a horse person, this was like dying and going to heaven.

By the time I paid for heavy equipment rentals, tools and supplies, between the move and the cost of construction, the checkbook said I was down to my last $25,000. I had to think of something to do to hold onto that last $25,000 to make it stretch. I couldn't use Chris' credit any more than I already had so I had to find someone else. Aha! I had the application for my apartment with my sister Debbie's personal information on it, so I would just use her credit, and before she figured out what happened, I would have everything paid off. I got an Amazon Visa card with a $2,500 balance and an American Express card with no limit. I purchased two brand-new laptop computers, one for myself and one for the ranch manager for his birthday, through a Dell credit line.

I celebrated Christmas with my friends at my ranch; it gave me a chance to show it off. Everyone was impressed and I was pleased. Blissfully happy. Totally unaware. I had no idea what was coming.

# CHAPTER 25
# A DATE WITH DESTINY
# 2008

I rang in New Year's on the Sunset Strip. I bought six tickets at $600 a pop to a private affair at a club called One. I drank way too much, at least a fifth of vodka a day. I was popping Xanax like Tic Tacs— between ten and twelve a day. If you add that up, it's 20 to 24mg per day, enough to tranquilize one of my horses. The tequila and the Xanax didn't mix right and soon after the clock struck midnight, we were all on our way back to the ranch. I was puking the entire way in a bucket we borrowed from the club. Not one of my finer moments, but not uncommon either.

The next weekend, I decided to meet Chris at a music industry show in Anaheim called the NAMM show, where musicians and suppliers of equipment got together every year and jammed. I rented a suite at one of the recommended hotels that was walking distance to the convention center. I don't know how much I paid—several hundred a night, I'm sure. I took a friend of mine (whose husband was also a musician) and my ranch manager, who just thought it was too good to be true because there were so many celebrities there. I took the ranch manager with me most of the time at this point because I was paranoid about being pulled over and arrested. I thought if someone else drove, got pulled over and showed their license, I, the passenger, would be off the hook. We had a great time. I was the perfect hostess and everything was on me, as usual.

The next weekend, I invited friends I met at the NAMM show over for a home-cooked meal at the ranch. It was a Sunday night. I made a traditional Italian dinner with my signature cheesecake for desert. A guy that I picked up at the NAMM show and was shacking up with that week wanted to know if he could marry me based on my cooking. I said he didn't know what he was asking and we laughed. That night, he stayed over and said he would take a ride with me in the morning to check in at my pretrial officer's office for my monthly visit. I thought, 'Hey that's great. I have a driver.'

It was Monday, January 28, 2008, and we'd had a torrential rain the day before with flooding. I called my pretrial officer and asked if I could reschedule and she said no, that I needed to make this appointment, and she couldn't accommodate me any other day that week. That I should just head on down to her office. I didn't take Louie, my Chihuahua, with me like I always did. I don't know if that was a sixth sense thing happening or what, but my friend and I left and headed downtown.

We got to the Roybal Federal Building and checked in. I had a 9am appointment, and when I was called back for my appointment, wham! Two US Marshalls came from behind the door, slapped a warrant down on the desk in front of me and said I was under arrest for a new indictment. My first reaction was *Ah, Florida*, so I said, "Florida?" They said, "No, California." My mind went blank . . . what exactly in California? Check fraud, credit card fraud, bank fraud, identity theft, racketeering, money laundering? The list of possibilities was endless . . . so in a very meek voice I said, "For what?" They replied, "Embezzlement." BINGO! The light bulb went off. My out-loud voice said, "Shit!" My inner voice said, "I'm screwed." My Long Beach lover's family went straight to the FBI. I wasn't surprised.

I was allowed to call my attorney John in Chicago and they took my personal belongings and said they would give them to my friend in the waiting room. I asked if I could take my medication and they said yes. I had six Xanax in a pill box in my purse, so I put them all in my hand and swallowed. They hurried me down an elevator in the back of the building that led to a garage where they had a car waiting to take me over to the Metropolitan Detention Center for booking. I had an arraignment scheduled for 1:30 that afternoon. I was booked and processed and sat in a holding cell by myself, feeling strangely calm. Of course I was calm—I had just taken 12mg of Xanax in one shot.

I had already discussed with John that it was impossible for him to appear in a few hours in Los Angeles, and I didn't want the arraignment held over because I was certain I would make bond and be able to fight this from home. So the federal defender put in appearance for him. I appeared before the Judge and was told it was his duty to sit in that chair and protect little old ladies from people like me. Bail was denied. I couldn't believe it; I had never stayed more than a few hours in jail. I explained to the judge that I had people who depended on me, animals that needed me, Hell, I needed to be medicated—they couldn't dispute this. All he said was, "You'll be allowed to make arrangements by phone and I hereby order your medication to be administered."

I was sent back to a holding cell where there were several other women being detained as well, and we all got to talking about what we did and why we were there. I remember one of the women saying, "Oh, so you're one of those smart criminals with money." I said, "No, not really. I'm just like you."

After several hours a female Marshall came and brought us up to the women's unit at MDC. It was about 11:00pm and lights were out and people were asleep. I was put in an available room, took my bed roll, made up the top bunk and passed out. I was drained and I needed to sleep off that Xanax.

I had no clue how prison worked. I may have been street-smart but I wasn't prison-smart. The next morning I was told I was in a "bad" room, so they moved me. One of the girls said she would show me the ropes and said I needed money on my books for the phone and commissary. I didn't even know what commissary was. She said, "Come on let's get you a phone call and a PAC number." I said, "What's that?" She said, "Everyone gets a PAC number—it's like a pin number so you can make calls, but you need to have money on your books first." I said, "How do I get money sent in?" She showed me how Western Union worked. I called the ranch and the manager answered and I told him where I had $12,000 hidden in the house—could he get it to Western Union and put it on my books? He said he would. He never did. That money disappeared. My next free call was to John and this is what he said: "You have a preliminary hearing on Friday at 9am and we're going to ask that your case be transferred to Chicago so we can combine it with your other indictment. I can handle the case since you've already retained me and I have been working on it for three years." I said, "No, I want another bond hearing. I want you to come out to California and get me a bond." And he said, "Chris, you are safer in prison than you are at home. You're staying right where you are. The time that you're doing now will count towards what you're sentenced with in the end." I didn't like it, but he had a point.

The federal defender helped me get in touch with my friend Carol in Vegas. I needed someone to get money on my books so I could use the phone and get deodorant, soap and toothpaste. They don't give you squat; you have to buy all of your toiletries and gym clothes or anything decent to eat yourself. The defender said he'd gotten a hold of her, and that evening she put $500 on my books. Every year Carol would send $500 and a birthday card, but she never took my calls. It was strange and I'd never understood it, but I appreciated the support. The next order of business was a power of attorney the ranch manager needed so he could place all of my animals in rescues. My heart was broken. I hadn't felt pain so palpable since my mother's death. I was supposed to keep them safe and I had abandoned them. At that moment, reality sunk in—I wasn't going anywhere and I panicked. I went completely bonkers, and kept repeating no, no, no, and I slammed my fists down on the attorney/client room table five or six times before the CO restrained me, shipped me back to the unit and put me in a lock-down cell by myself until I calmed down. The next day, I started to have withdrawals from my Xanax and they isolated me while I fought the withdrawal. I went through withdrawal for two weeks. I thought I was going to die. Vomiting, the shakes, the sweats. I would hear things—dogs barking, phones ringing, familiar sounds. When I faded in and out, I wasn't sure if I was home or if I was still in prison. I finally was well enough to be out in population with my fellow inmates and that evening I was sprung from lock-down. I heard, "Favara, pill line." I said to the girls, "What are they talking about?" and a girl said, "You gotta go up there and get your skittles." I just looked at her. She said, "Your psych meds, bitch. You wanna sleep, right?" Damn right, I wanted to sleep. There's no way I wanted to be awake for more hours than I had to be in this place. And there was the beginning of my compliance with my medication. The doctor hooked me up with 1200mg of Lithium, 60mg of Prozac and 80mg of Geodon to replace the Xanax, and from that night on, I slept like a baby and never missed a call for pill line.

The judge in Sacramento ordered me to appear on the indictment even though it was being rolled up in Chicago, so I was put on "in transit" status and started my journey to Chicago. The first stop was a week's stay in the San Bernardino County Jail. I was then transferred in shackles and handcuffs for 13 hours to the lovely Sacramento County Main Jail, rated the third worst jail in the country at that time. I appeared in front of the judge in Sacramento and it was ordered to send me on to Chicago. It would be another two weeks and another prison change to Nevada City before I was on the airlift, better known as "ConAir," to Chicago.

ConAir was frightening. I couldn't decide which was worse: being on a plane with a bunch of hungry men that were sex-starved, or being handcuffed and shackled and not being able to save yourself in the event of a crash. Needless to say, if they would have let me kiss the ground when I got off, I would have. We got to Chicago and the Metropolitan Correctional Center bus had a few of us to take back to the prison. By this time, I had become used to being booked and processed, with this being my fifth jail. I went through the whole long, tedious process of getting uniforms, underwear, bra, socks and shoes, and going over my medication with the PA. I was finally sent up to the women's unit. It must have been after midnight. I was assigned to a four-man dorm and I was exhausted so I just passed out, after I was dispensed my medication, of course. I was on it now—meds meant sleep. No meds, no sleep. It was that simple. I really didn't care about being compliant more than I cared about not being awake and left to face my own demons at night.

I realized quickly that all of the so-called "friends" I had were just along for the ride. They got what they could when they could. By now, all that I had been hiding was out in the open and those that weren't afraid of me were furious. I had no one. No one to call, no one to write. I had no cell phone. All of my numbers were in my cell phone and only a few were memorized, but who wanted to talk to me? But there was one person—my friend Eric. He had always been a rock and I gave it a try and he took my call and was my biggest cheerleader during the time up until my sentencing. He sent books, magazines, newspapers, money. A good friend. I will always be grateful for how kind he was to me. He even visited a few times when I was in Chicago—his mom lived about three hours away and if he went to visit her, he came to see me. Sweet. The only person's address I could remember was Loretta's; although 29 years had passed, I still remember it now. I sat and wrote her a letter telling her what happened and asked if she could forgive me for being a horrible friend. In my heart, I knew she would be the one person who wouldn't judge me and I was right. A couple of weeks later, at mail call, I got a letter. I knew her handwriting instantly and I cried. In her letter, she included her number and that night started the first of monthly calls to Loretta from prison.

I spoke to John by phone weekly and, on this particular call, he told me that the original owner of the ranch had gone there to clean up and was nice enough to gather a box together of some of my personal belongings—pictures mostly and some stuff I had saved over the years. I asked if it would be okay if she shipped them to his office and held on to them for me. Another box was sent to him from MDC Los Angeles, which contained the clothes I was arrested in: jeans, a t-shirt, a pair of boots, my undergarments and a denim jacket. When I hung up, I realized that after all the money I spent, all of the expensive things I purchased, out of all of my possessions . . . I was reduced to everything fitting into two boxes. A sobering reality.

I accepted my plea on July 11, 2008. We finally agreed that I would plead guilty to Stock Market Manipulation in Illinois and Florida, with restitution previously paid in the civil judgment the SEC gave me in 2005, and they would throw out the California indictment. However I had to agree to pay back the $155,000 I stole in the form of restitution. I balked at the restitution, but John said to take the deal so I took it.

After you take your plea, the official pre-sentencing process begins. The Department of Justice and probation conduct what they call a PSI—Pre-Sentencing Investigation. It's a report that is based on a lengthy interview with the defendant and then your family to verify your history and if what you say is in fact true. They also pull a credit report and check for any other criminal records, old or new. They then decide how many points you're worth—the federal system is based on points. So many points, plus your criminal history category range, equal how much time you are sentenced under the guidelines. This report, along with a recommendation, is submitted to the judge for his consideration prior to your sentencing to help provide the judge with the background that he needs to make his decision. An added component to my PSI was that I underwent a psych evaluation from a neutral third party; John insisted we not have the quacks at MCC do the evaluation. Wise move. Dr. Carl Whalstrom spent about three hours with me and determined that all three of my previous doctors were correct. After carefully reviewing my medical records, and based on his own findings, I was classified as Bipolar I and required rehabilitation. Gee, ya think? I remember one thing that he was perplexed about. My PSI stated that I donated either with time or in money to over 57 charities. He asked if I could explain why I was so charitable and I told him that sometimes, there are two of me: the person that is a criminal and another that is a Christian, and sometimes, I have a hard time choosing between the two.

When the PSI process was over, I went back to my cell and thought, Great, I need my story verified. How are they supposed to do that? I didn't speak to my family. No one had been in contact with me, and I wasn't in contact with them. How would probation verify my story? Now what? I did the only thing I could do; I swallowed my pride and called my sister Debbie. It had been seven months since we'd last spoken and I had no idea what I was going to say, and moreover, how she was going to react. So I asked the counselor if I could have some privacy and call from his phone in his office and he said no problem. I still, to this day, do not understand how she contained herself from telling me to drop dead. She was very, very happy to hear from me and was concerned for my safety and if I was okay and how I was doing. She told me she knew about my being bipolar and asked if I was taking my medication and I told her that I was fine. I explained to her that life was so out of control that coming to prison saved my life. I would have either overdosed or wrecked my car, and this was forcing me to get well. She was very supportive and I explained about the probation department's needing to verify my family history and she agreed to talk to them. I asked her if it would be alright if I stayed in touch and called her. And she said of course—that she really wanted me to and that she loved me. She never mentioned anything about what I'd done to her, and when I brought it up, she said it was in the past and to move on, so we did. And so began monthly calls and letters to my sister.

The Chaplin said we were allowed to make calls from his office to our own pastors at home if we wished, so I wrote Father Michael, a dear, long-time friend from my parish, Blessed Sacrament, in Los Angeles. I explained what happened in the letter, at which he was not surprised. I had confided in him many times, and asked him if he would take my call, and he did. And so began quarterly spiritual calls to him from prison.

Those first few months, I learned the meaning of what they were teaching us in the AA meetings I was attending: acceptance. Acceptance of my actions and my medication. I learned the true meaning of forgiveness—forgiveness from others and forgiveness of myself.

# ACCEPTANCE

And acceptance is the answer to all my problems today. When I am disturbed it is because I find some person, place, things or situation—some fact of my life unacceptable to me, and I can find no serenity until I accept that person, place, thing or situation as being exactly the way it is supposed to be at this moment. Nothing, absolutely nothing, happens in God's world by mistake. Unless I accept life completely on life's terms, I cannot be happy. I need to concentrate not so much on what needs to be changed in the world as on what needs to be changes in me and in my attitudes.

—Alcoholics Anonymous

# CHAPTER 26
# TIME IS ON MY SIDE, YES, IT IS
# 2009

I had been in prison a year. My weight spiked, as it always did when I took my medication, and I was weighing in at about 210 pounds. It's easy to do when you stuff your face all day with crap from commissary and you're horizontal most of the time, with the exception of watching TV and going to the rooftop or the gym once a week. There was nothing else to do. I read and wrote. I was a voracious reader—I could read a book in one day. I counted before I left prison (I used the Amazon receipts I saved that came with the books in the mail), and I'd read 320 books, not counting what I took out of the library. I was better read in prison than I was outside of it; on top of books, I browsed magazines and newspapers. I would pout if my Wall Street Journal didn't show up. It was these simple things I looked forward to . . . amazing how your priorities change.

Anyone in prison waiting to be sentenced can tell you the longest waits are: one, for the results of your PSI, and two, the day you're actually sentenced. Finally, I received my recommendations back on my PSI in March. I had 26 points with a criminal history category of one, which put me a guideline range of being committed for 70–78 months. I had already done ten months, which meant I had 68 months to go if the judge sentenced me at the high end and 60 at the low end. Five or more years. I was devastated. The only thing I could pray for at this point was that the judge would take my drug abuse and drinking into consideration and give me RDAP (Residential Drug Abuse Program), and I could get up to 18 months off of my sentence. John said he would ask for it and my PSI contained the proof that I did in fact have a dependency issue. All I could do at this point was do my time.

The months between March and June just dragged along. I had myself and everyone else convinced that I would serve time, that the judge would be lenient because of my mental health. Eric was making plans for me to come back to California and move in with him, and we talked about how we were going to love and cherish each other. Friends, this was all fantasy. Wishful thinking on both our parts. After the sentencing, I never talked to Eric again.

June 9, 2009, 11am. I stood before Judge Blanche Manning and waited for my sentence. John and the Assistant US Attorney saw to the formalities and then I was on—time for me to deliver my speech. Oh, sure—Loretta, my sister Debbie, and my dear friend Father Michael (my Pastor from Los Angeles) wrote letters on my behalf, but she wanted to hear from me. I stood there and told her how very sorry I was, that I wasn't in the right frame of mind for many years and did things that were uncharacteristic and that I was regretful. She didn't buy it. She said, "You know what, Ms. Favara? That's a nice speech you prepared but you don't seem very remorseful." Everything she said after that fell on deaf ears. The next things I heard were 78 months, three years supervised release, mandatory mental health counseling and medication monitoring, as part of the conditions of my supervised release, and I was to pay the restitution of $155,000 at 10% of my income per month. No RDAP. Holy shit. That didn't go exactly as I had hoped.

That night I reported the bad news to everyone, and they were in a state of disbelief. I passed on supper that night and lay in my bunk and cried. My sister did say that my nephew Mike was asking about me and she gave me his number. He said to call him; he wanted to talk and see how I was. No problem. I called him that evening and I remember he turned a bad day around. It was nice to know there was one more person that cared.

The next morning, I heard, "Favara, legal visit." I figured John came by to give me his best, and then he told me there was an error in my sentencing. I had to go back next week and be resentenced, and I said, "Mistake good or mistake bad?" He said, "Mistake, good . . . she's resentencing you to 70 months with the RDAP requirement." YES! Redemption.

Not long after you're sentenced, you are designated to leave the holding facility that you're in and actually go to a federal prison of an FCI (as they are called). I was designated to Danbury, and sent to a medium security prison behind a barbed wire fence. I didn't get to go to Camp Cupcake like Martha Stewart. All federal inmates go through Oklahoma, which is the main central hub for transferring, so I boarded ConAir and sat in Oklahoma for a few days before I was flown back on ConAir to Danbury.

I got to Danbury in October and I was so excited to be out in the fresh air that I spent hours out in the rec yard walking the track; I was going to get this weight off of me one way or another. It took a few days to get the routine down and figure out how things operate because every prison has its own hierarchy and protocol. I was in unit 11 when I first got there, which had stairs, the likes I hadn't seen since the Statue of Liberty on the inside. It was a workout just to climb all 32 of those every time you wanted to go in and out. I walked out to go to the rec yard and I couldn't believe my eyes: it was a dog, a yellow lab named Suki, a prison-trained dog to be used in the ATF. It was the first time I had seen or touched an animal in 21 months. I got choked up when she licked me. Her handler (my friend Donna) said I should enroll in the Puppies Behind Bars program, but she said you had to be strict, and everyone knew I was a sucker when it came to animals and I would want them to sleep in my bunk. So I didn't do it—I just enjoyed the ones on the compound.

You got assigned a job when you went to prison and had the privilege of making $0.23 per hour. I worked the mandatory three months in the kitchen doing dishes, and then I worked in education teaching the GED and ESL classes. At night, I would donate my time to other inmates that needed legal help at the law library. I also worked the yard at night, which meant I swept, shoveled snow, mowed, raked leaves—that kind of stuff. Anything to not be stuck in the unit. When I was in the unit, I read. I had given up TV totally; it was too much of a headache fighting over channels and saving seats. Kindergarten crap.

I met some good people when I was in prison, believe it or not—some I even talk with today. There were always three or four girls I regularly hung out with and we took care of one another. Bought each other stuff, played board games, cards. Yahtzee was my favorite. Whatever we could do to pass the time. I never opened up much to anybody in prison, with the exception of my roommate Lindsay in Chicago, whom I still stay in touch with today. She was the only one who really ever knew any of my secrets and fears. For the most part, I kept to myself and would always help if I could and be charitable if someone didn't have what I did. I made sure they got what they needed. I was trying to even my karmic scales. Everyone in prison figures out what the best way is for them to pass the time; this is how I passed mine.

# CHAPTER 27
# WHAT HAPPENS IN VEGAS
# DOESN'T ALWAYS STAY
# THERE
# 2010

I had been in prison two years and six months by the time I was eligible to apply for the RDAP program. I was called to the Director of the program's office and she conducted an intake interview. She asked simple questions, really. Did I drink and use Xanax the way it indicated in my PSI? Why did I want the RDAP program? I told her the truth: one, I want the 18 months off, and two, I understand you have mental health counseling as a component and I need it. She listened and said I had one problem. I couldn't imagine what it was. She said, "You have three detainers for additional state cases that are pending charges." My eyes grew wide and I could feel myself get pale and I said, "For what?" She said she didn't know the particulars but to report to Records and they would explain. In the meantime, she couldn't admit me to the program until the detainers were cleared up. I went to the next open house that week at

Records to find out what the hell was going on. I mean, I'm in prison—how much more trouble could I get in?

The officer in charge of my case said I had a detainer from the State of Nevada for unpaid casino markers, a second from the Palm Beach County, Florida Sheriff's Department for identity theft, and a third from the San Fernando Police Department in Los Angeles for credit card fraud. Oh, wow. I was in more trouble.

I went immediately to my unit and called John, almost in tears, and he said to give him a few days, let him make some calls and get a handle on it. A week later, I called him back and he spoke music to my ears. He was able to have the two charges in Palm Beach and San Fernando dismissed; however, Vegas would only consent to charging me and running my sentence of one year concurrently, which meant while I did my federal time, it would count as state time as well. This was the best possible outcome.

I went back to Records with the disposition of all the charges, and a week later, I got my acceptance to the RDAP program. This meant my sentence would be shortened by 18 months. Proof once again that God is indeed good. In October I moved to my new unit, which housed the RDAP program 12L, the move that would make me face my demons and come to terms with my disease.

On my first day, I got assigned my room and met my counselor. I had no idea this woman would become my confidante, the voice of reason and the person I hear in my head today. She was the first person in the 22 months I had been in prison that sat, listened, talked and asked tough questions and made me dig down deep and soul-search. We met weekly for an hour in her office for nine months. She got to the root of my problems and together, we put me back together.

What I thought was a bullshit way to get 18 months off became the most difficult experience of my life. The rules were tougher in this unit than on the rest of the compound—you got held to a higher standard here. We spent mornings and evenings doing our jobs and our own thing, but from noon to 4pm, you programmed. RDAP is not rehab; it is a program designed to change your way of thinking. What led you to become addicted? What led you to your criminal path, and what are you going to do differently when you leave this controlled environment? Now, this could go either way: you could either immerse yourself in the program and learn from it, or you could just pretend to learn something from it. I chose to learn something. I may not have been the most vocal in class but I absorbed and pondered and analyzed. And I figured out what my problems were and I fixed them. I'm not saying I'm perfect. I am saying I'm better. You ask yourself, what's different this time? This time I was ready. Acceptance, my friends. Acceptance.

# Part VI

# It's Finally Over, Or Is It?

*"I KNOW GOD WILL NOT GIVE ME ANYTHING I CAN'T HANDLE. I JUST WISH HE DIDN'T TRUST ME SO MUCH."*

—MOTHER THERESA

# CHAPTER 28
# I'M FREE, SO TO SPEAK
# 2011

I t was January and the countdown began. Seven months and 23 days until I was released. My case manager called me and said it was time. He sent my release package to the halfway house where I'd be going. In my heart, I wanted to return to California, but the new and improved Christine said, "I don't know. Let me check with my family and I will get back to you." That evening, I called Loretta and asked if it would be okay if I came to Virginia, and I held my breath while she thought about it. I expected a no, but just as my friend always has, she believed in me and wanted the best, and she wanted me to have a second chance, so she said yes. We didn't work out particulars but at least I knew where I was headed. I spoke to my family and I told them what had been decided, and everyone, especially my nephew, was overjoyed with my decision and said I was welcomed there. So my nephew Mike (who, if you remember, used to visit Virginia as I did when we were kids) said he would pick me up upon my release and bring me to Virginia. I was getting excited. It may have been months away but I knew the end was in sight. I could see the light at the end of the tunnel.

By March, it was time for Virginia probation to do a home check at Loretta's. I wasn't at all worried—Loretta and her family are solid, Christian people who are stable, unlike yours truly. The report came back clear: it was a go. My halfway house package was approved and I could be released to Virginia. I called and let everyone know. Mike told me that his twin brother Joe was happy for me and asked to speak to me. I called Joe that evening and we caught up and reminisced as much as you can on a 15-minute-maximum phone call and he said that he would meet up with Mike and, together, they would drive me to the halfway house. It was a date.

The night before my release, I weighed myself in the gym. I was exactly 150 pounds, the same weight I'd been when I came in. I had lost all the weight I gained in Chicago. I packed a box of things I needed to take: my legal paperwork, toiletries, my bible and journals. Waiting for me in discharge (or R&D, as we call it) was what my sister sent so I didn't have to wear my grays out: a bra, underwear, shirt, pants, sneakers and a jacket. She also included a $100 Visa gift card and a calling card. I had my hair flat-ironed by my roommate Jen, a great girl from Baltimore. We had really bonded over those nine months together in the program and still keep in touch today. I primped as much as you can in prison and then went to pill line, like I had every other night for the last 43 months, so that I could take my medication and get a good night's sleep. Sleep never came. I watched the sunrise for the last time over FCI Danbury and it was glorious.

On August 23, 2011, I was discharged. It was the weirdest feeling in the world. I am not sure I can describe it properly. I was in real clothes and held real money in my hands. They gave me the balance that was on my books: $50. Then they opened the door and I walked through. They said, "Your family is waiting in the lobby." When I saw my nephews, I froze. I thought I would be overwhelmed and cry and kiss the ground, but I was unsure of how to act so I froze. Then I realized, oh, yeah, stupid, give them a hug. And I hugged them and kissed them and probably held a little tighter and longer than they wanted, but it felt good.

It was an 11-hour drive from Danbury to the halfway house in Norfolk, Virginia. We stopped in Staten Island and got a bite to eat at a diner we used to go to when we were teenagers, and my first meal out of prison was a bagel and lox with a glass of orange juice. I remember my nephews laughed when I sighed after taking my first sip of fresh-squeezed orange juice. We dropped Joe off at his home and said hi to his wife and oldest son and then Mike and I drove on. We caught up during our trip on the family and all the many changes. He didn't ask me what happened or what led me to prison; I hope this book answers all the questions that went unanswered for years. We said our goodbyes as he left me in the hallway and handed me $40 and told me to call him in a couple of days and let him know how it was going. I gave him another big hug and kiss and I stepped into the next phase of my life - re-entry back into society.

The halfway house was modest, not much different from prison. Crappy food, and you still had to share a room. You did get a door on the bathroom; now that, I must say, was a novelty for a while. Within a few days after orientation, you are given a pass so you can go to a store and get personal items: toiletries, laundry detergent, clothes. I took my first trip as a free woman to Wal-Mart. I wanted to go crazy but I had a limited budget so I got necessities. For me, these were toiletries, underwear, laundry supplies, a purse, a wallet and a bottle of perfume. You are only allowed scented oil in prison, so real perfume was a "must have."

The phones are not restricted at the halfway house like they are in prison, and there is no recording that asks you if you will accept the call and press "5". I was able to catch up with some friends in LA that I hadn't spoken to while I was gone and that was nice. Next was the phone call I had been waiting to make the entire time I was gone. I called Chris. He knew who it was immediately and I said my peace. I told him how disappointed I was that he didn't get in touch with me or help me after all I had done for him, that I expected him, out of all the people in my life, to stand by me. And that's when he unloaded. Apparently, when I went to prison, everyone thought Chris knew everything I was doing and was a part of it. He said that it took almost a year before the fighting with people was over. Then he spent the next year trying to clean up the aftermath of the mess I left behind. He said there was a part of him that didn't want to have anything to do with me ever again and then there was a part of him that felt guilty and sorry, but he was too afraid to contact me. I said I understood and we hung up the phone and parted as friends. We still keep in touch today.

I called John to let him know I made it to the halfway house. At this point, he was a friend more than he was an attorney, and as any good friend would, he cared about my wellbeing. He was happy I was out and gave me his best. I asked him to please send me boxes that he'd been holding this whole time to Loretta's—that I would need the clothes and, of course, I wanted to see for myself exactly what was in the box from the ranch. He sent everything to Loretta's and she would hold onto them until I got there.

You are required to work when you are in the halfway house, and pay 25% of your earnings in the form of rent. I got a job making minimum wage at a telemarketing company in Virginia Beach. It was great to be out and doing things in the everyday world. I would get passes to be out for free time and I would go to the library or a coffee shop or the dollar store. I remember my first Starbucks—it was heaven. The halfway house wasn't so bad; I mean, anything beat prison. But it's like you're free during the day when you're at work or on a pass and then you're in prison at night. You couldn't get too comfortable because you were still in a controlled environment.

Part of the requirement when you're released from RDAP is that you continue your counseling during the term of your halfway house stay, so I went once a week for group and once a week for a one-on-one session. I was pleased with the counselor they gave me—I really felt we connected and that I was getting the support I needed. In total, I would spend six months at the halfway house and during that time, I would be taking the steps to prepare for living in the real world again. What I didn't realize was how difficult of a transition this would actually be.

My sisters Debbie and Susie, as well as Loretta, sent care packages, clothes, and toiletries—things I found to be comforting. I remember Loretta sent slippers and Dove soap for my birthday and I was over the moon that I had real soap and not the cheap bar stuff they sold in prisons. Loretta's younger brother Daniel was in Virginia Beach for the weekend and came by and saw me. It was nice to have a visitor. Loretta sent my clothes that were shipped to John from prison so long ago, and I was thrilled I had expensive stuff in there: all of my Gap attire, La Perla undergarments, and a pair of Harley Davidson boots. It would certainly beat the thrift store clothes I was wearing. When I tried them on, they hung on me and I didn't feel comfortable. In some respects, they weren't me anymore; they just didn't suit me. And that's when I realized I had changed.

# CHAPTER 29
# IT'S LIKE RIDING A HORSE
# 2012

I made it through the halfway house—my six months were up. I was released from the halfway house at 10am on February 28, 2012 and the first thing I did was go to a local restaurant where we used to hang out and have my first adult beverage—a vodka and cranberry juice. I know what you're thinking already—I fell off the wagon. No, sir. I had just one drink and I didn't even finish it. I just did it because it seemed like I should celebrate with my friends and consummate the whole "being free" thing.

The friends I made in Norfolk drove me to the Greyhound station in Richmond and I boarded the bus to Charlottesville. My two-hour ride was spent trying to calm the butterflies in my stomach. I was nervous to see Loretta after 23 years. She had only been a voice over the phone the last 49 months. Loretta's husband Tim picked me up at the bus depot (she was at a basketball game for her son Michael). After we hugged, Tim took me to finally see Loretta, and the anticipation was killing me. Then, finally, there she was, just as I remembered. A tad bit older, but nonetheless the same person. I remember how good it felt to finally hold her, and in that moment, I knew I was home.

That night, we stayed up talking like school girls. I was excited and am sure I talked fast and furiously. Over the next week that I stayed with Loretta and her family, we reminisced and went out to eat and did all the fun stuff you do in the real world.

In the morning I went out and took a look around. I came in at night and I wasn't able to see my surroundings. Everything was as I remembered it. It was as if time had stood still. It was comforting to know that some people and places hadn't changed, yet I realized that this world was way different from the one I had left in 2008.

I met my probation officer that afternoon, and as luck would have it, God blessed me with a good one. A good Christian man concerned about my rehabilitation mentally and my re-entry into society. We went over the standard conditions of release, which were: don't do drugs, don't possess a firearm, don't commit a crime, and don't travel outside of your jurisdiction without permission. Of course I had some special conditions: make my restitution payments at 10% of my income per month and do not open any lines of credit or obtain any credit cards. I then took a drug test and I was out the door.

That evening, Loretta gave me my boxes. She had since placed everything in plastic storage bins, but the contents were the same. And there it was—all that was left of my former life. I was connected yet removed. I saw faces in pictures of people I missed. It was bittersweet.

About a week after staying at Loretta's, the Overholt's were generous enough to allow me to move into a house on their property. I now had the pleasure of living in a three-bedroom farmhouse circa 1930s, on 36 open acres in Aroda, Virginia, just a mile from their farm that I'd grown up on and visited when I was a child through the Fresh Air Fund.

I was getting myself on my feet and was in the process of getting my license back and picking up things for the house. A dog and a horse were the first order of priority. I decided to take a stab at finding someone to date (I was ready and long overdue if you know what I mean), so I turned to my trusty friend, the dating authority Craigslist, and posted an ad for a soul mate. My ad said I wanted someone I could do everything with and they must love animals and not be interested in a one-night stand. I got creepy offers and I talked to a couple of people, but no one tickled my fancy until Stevie answered my ad. After a couple of emails back and forth, we decided to talk over the phone. We stayed up like teenagers that night and talked until, like, 3am . . . and we made plans for him to come over the next night for margaritas.

On March 26, 2012, Stevie walked into my life and he has been here ever since. A handsome, adorable man, I thought, with just the right amount of gray in his hair. I laid it on him the first night; hi, thanks for coming, I am an ex-con and am bipolar—still want to stay? But he didn't flinch, said everyone had baggage and I was no different, and it wasn't for him to judge me. Stevie and I are definitely polar opposites, no pun intended. He is a hillbilly and I am a city slicker, but we love each other unconditionally and that works for us.

We spent that month getting to know each other and then he moved in. We began accumulating stuff: furniture, animals. Of course I was doing rescue every chance I got and, to date, we have four dogs, six cats, two horses and Kiwi. In April I had a special delivery arrive that had to be picked up at the airport. I had tracked down most of my animals and asked if they were well when I was released. It was just that I had to hear it for myself that they were fine and happy—it was important to me. Kiwi, my parrot, had gone to stay with one of my volunteers from the rescue, and when I contacted Nancy, she said she would be happy to send Kiwi to me if I wanted him. The plans were made and Kiwi was sent. It was an emotional reunion, as he was the only animal I was able to keep after all this time, my only link to that part of my life. I was overwhelmed and grateful to have him back.

I finally got a job and worked steadily for a couple of months, but it just didn't work out. In fact, I had several jobs during that year that didn't work out. The jobs that accepted my background sucked and the ones that were worth anything wouldn't overlook the fact that I had committed a serious financial crime. I just thought it would get better with time, and I would be able to find something eventually. I kept my chin up.

In May, after all the appropriate court paperwork went through, I began my monthly medication supervision and therapy sessions with Dr. Jennifer Oldham and Laurel Hillstrom of Behavioral Healthcare Community Service. I was pessimistic at best; I figured court-ordered doctors equaled quacks. But I was proven wrong. To date I am pleased with their treatment and feel that they "get" me. Dr. Oldham continued my medication regimen of 1200mg of Lithium and 60mg of Prozac, and changed my sleep medication from 80mg of Geodon to 10mg of Saphris, which worked. I was pleased. The most important thing about therapy is that you feel a connection to the person to whom you are baring your soul.

By the middle of August I was depressed. I couldn't think straight and everything in my brain was cloudy, a telltale sign of hypomania. I hadn't had a manic or depressed mood in four-and-a-half years and it hit me like a ton of bricks. The trigger, you ask? There's always a trigger. Financially, we weren't making it, and I tipped the scales at 250 pounds. I couldn't get a job anywhere. I felt like I was a failure and would never get through this. The life plans I was making weren't working out. I over-extended myself. I had corporate tax debt that caught up with me. My payroll checks from a company I was working for bounced, and I owed the check-cashing place I had used the money. My checking account was overdrawn, with legitimate reason this time, and the checks I wrote to others to pay for goods and services were bouncing. The snowball started to get bigger and bigger. I was doing it again and I had to stop myself before someone got hurt.

I called Dr. Oldham and Laurel and immediately went in for counseling. I got myself back on track after a few weeks. By the end of August I felt somewhat normal. Then I got a call during the last weekend in August. Loretta called to say their family dog Buster was involved in a hit-

and-run the day before and asked if I could go over and help the boys clean out the cut. I went over and I couldn't believe the dog was still alive. This wasn't a cut; this was a mess. I knew instantly it was bad—everything in the leg was exposed—arteries, veins, cartilage, bone. I knew it was going to be a miracle if we saved his life, let alone his leg. I did what I knew how to do from being in rescue for so many years: I packed his leg with a wet dressing and posted for any help anyone could provide on Craigslist. No one answered. I let a day go by, but I knew I was running out of time so I contacted a rescue in Los Angeles who had placed all of my dogs when I went to prison and asked if they could help. They said, "Do whatever you need to do to save the dog and we'll support you." Sunday evening, I took Buster to an emergency vet, who kept him overnight and repacked his wound just like I did. He would be transported to a different vet in the morning to perform the amputation. We now had a bill at the emergency vet for $1,033. The plan was that I would write the checks at the time the services were performed and then the rescue in LA would reimburse me. Three days later, the final bill from the second vet was $2,397. When I called and explained the precarious situation to the director of the rescue, all she could say was they had their own financial problems at this time and they were sorry, but they couldn't honor their commitment. Yikes. I was majorly screwed. The rescue never covered those checks. I was on the hook. I called a local St. Bernard rescue, since Buster was a St. Bernard mix, and they said they would cover what the rescue in LA didn't, but they never did. I called both vets, who seemed sympathetic, but the bottom line was they wanted their money. Both vets sent me to collections—the same collections company—and the collection company in turn got in touch with me and made a formal demand in October for payment in writing. I called to set up a payment arrangement and I was told that he didn't make deals. He prosecuted. I was a sitting duck.

On Sunday, November 18, 2012, I was arrested at my home at 7:30pm on felony check charges. Of course Stevie came to my rescue and he and his brother bailed me out and got me an attorney, but here I was, back in trouble again. "This can't be happening" was all I could say to myself in the back of the Madison County Sheriff's patrol car that night.

I was taken to Orange County Regional Jail for processing and detention. I would require a bond. I was placed in a holding cell. I was alone on the hard concrete floor with a steel bed frame and a thin pad they called a mattress and the aesthetically pleasing metal toilet with no paper to wipe. I said to myself, "You can't do this, you can't live in the past, and the people you knew are not your friends. That old life has no place in the here and now. You're not the average bear; you have more to lose than everybody else. If you don't stop what you're doing, this is where you will end up for the rest of your life." And I cried. About 2:00am, I was released on a $3,000 bond. When I saw Stevie, I clung to him.

I reported the incident, as I was required to within 72 hours as per the conditions of my release; I, of course, waited until hour 71, fearful of the repercussions. My PO was disappointed. He said, "You're not in violation until we know the disposition of this case so keep me posted and we'll discuss your options when the time comes." Great, more waiting. I was physically sick. All the old feelings of going through my entire pleading out and being sentenced in Chicago came back and I didn't like this feeling, I didn't have it in me anymore. I couldn't do it and more importantly I didn't want to live like this anymore.

I hired an attorney, a real slime ball, who was later replaced by the public defender. If that doesn't tell you how horrible he was, nothing else will. My attorney made a deal with the Commonwealth's attorney that if I paid the checks in full before my court date on March 19, 2013, they would drop the charges. Hallelujah, there is indeed a God! Not that I ever had any doubts.

# Chapter 30
# A Cat Has Nine Lives and Always Lands on its Feet
# 2013

I busted my ass to make those payments and had some help in the end from some dear friends of mine. March 19, 2013 rolled around and I appeared and they told me the best they could do was drop it to a misdemeanor. This wasn't good. That meant I had violated, and a violation meant I would be sent back to prison. I called my PO from the courthouse and he said I needed to email him the disposition and then he needed some time to decide what they were going to do about the violation. He thought, at this point, I may just be able to get house arrest for 60 days, but he wasn't sure, and the other option he tossed around was three weekends in jail. Neither sufficed. A week later, he let me know I would have to see the judge because it was a Class B violation, which meant a guideline of a return to prison for four to ten months.

I called John in Chicago immediately. He looked into coming out to handle it, but it made more sense to go with the federal defender, the court-appointed Andrea Harris, who did an outstanding job. She knew the players and she knew the system, which made me extremely comfortable.

My PO violated me on two issues: one, that I had been convicted of a crime while on supervised release, and two, that during the last year, I had not made any restitution payments. They set a bond hearing for June 6th at 9:30am and I was officially served the request of the honor of my presence by US Marshall at my home two weeks prior. I made bond and my preliminary hearing was set for July 10, 2013 at 11am.

I really had to ask myself at this point: is it that I am bipolar, and have no impulse control sometimes? Or was I just stupid? I know my heart was in the right place. I wanted to do something to pay Loretta back for all she had done for me, but at what cost? My attorney Andrea seemed confident that due to the mitigating factors, and the fact that I paid the checks off, I stood a good chance at not being sent back, but anyone who has been through the system like I had known this was a crap shoot . . . 50/50 chance, at best. I prayed. That's all I could do.

On July 10, 2013, I caught the biggest break of my life. Judge Conrad was not pleased about the conviction and was even less pleased about the issue of the restitution, but he felt I was making an honest effort in all other areas and my heart was in the right place and it wasn't malicious. He re-sentenced me to an additional two years supervised release and re-imposed my original restitution. Of course there were court assessments (fines), but I couldn't squabble over a few pennies, when I still had my freedom.

You're asking, why didn't you just put the dog down? All this risk and heartache to save a dog? It's just a dog, you say. I ask you to keep these words I live by in mind. It's a life, and every life is worth saving. A poet that I admire, Jim Willis, says it best: "If you consider that we cannot save them all, and what difference does one make? You ought to know the joy of the one who is saved." Take it from me—I'm living proof.

# Epilogue

*"THE PAST CANNOT BE CHANGED,
THE FUTURE IS YET IN YOUR POWER.
IT'S NEVER TOO LATE TO BECOME
THE PERSON YOU MIGHT HAVE BEEN."*
*—GEORGE ELLIOT*

I decided to write a book while I was in prison, and when I came home, I kept putting it off because I didn't have my happy ending. I'm not so sure that happy endings exist like they do in fairy tales, but I am content with this unfinished life. When I sat down to write I found it liberating and therapeutic. I confirmed that I was a survivor and not a victim. I realized that I've learned to give not because I have had so much, but because I know exactly how it feels to have nothing. I have loved every minute I have spent putting my experiences down on paper with the hopes that someone may read this and learn from my mistakes or identify with some of my behavior and decide they need professional help. I am also hopeful that I have answered the questions that my family has been too afraid to ask. I have often been asked: Would have I done things differently? Wouldn't I choose not to be Bipolar? Of course. I am sure I could have made better decisions, but in retrospect, all of these events have somehow amazingly defined my character and made me who I am today. I may not be who I ought to be. I know I am not all that I want to be. But I've come a long way from who I used to be. And I won't give up on becoming what I know I can be. I often try to imagine what my life would have been like had my parents not died—would all the subsequent events not have taken place or was it fate or destiny? And was this the path that God had already laid out for me? Hard to say. All I do know is that their deaths set in motion a chain reaction that made me forever different.

"The ultimate lesson all of us
have to learn is unconditional love,
which includes not only others but
ourselves as well."

—Elizabeth Kubler-Ross

Made in the USA
Monee, IL
21 February 2022

91610502R00105